A teenage bride an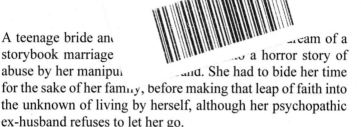..eam of a
storybook marriage _..o a horror story of
abuse by her manipu. _..id. She had to bide her time
for the sake of her famiiy, before making that leap of faith into
the unknown of living by herself, although her psychopathic
ex-husband refuses to let her go.

Thus, she proved to herself and others that not only it can
be done, but, for the sake of health and sanity, it has to be
done.

Determined to help others, she wrote this novel from the
heart in the hope that anyone who is being subjugated and
oppressed, will gain the determination to escape that secret,
black, evil environment. Divorced for five years, Constance
Turner is now independent, free-spirited, very happy and
proud of her survival.

I would like to dedicate this book to all survivors who live to tell their story…

Constance Turner

IF I CAN, YOU CAN!

AUSTIN MACAULEY PUBLISHERS™

LONDON • CAMBRIDGE • NEW YORK • SHARJAH

Author's Note: I have tried to recreate events, locales and conversations from my memories of them. In order to maintain their anonymity in some instances I have changed the names of individuals and places, I may have changed some identifying characteristics and details such as physical properties, occupations and places of residence.

A CIP catalogue record for this title is available from the British Library.

ISBN 9781528999502 (Paperback)
ISBN 9781528999519 (ePub e-book)

www.austinmacauley.com

First Published (2020)
Austin Macauley Publishers Ltd
25 Canada Square
Canary Wharf
London
E14 5LQ

I would like to thank Lynne Heraud for allowing me to use the phrase from one of her amazing songs, *The Working Man*.

'We've been constrained too much, too long,

And now we've left our cage…'

Table of Contents

"Life owes me nothing

One clear morn is boon enough
For being born

And, be it ninety years—or ten
No need for me to question when,

My life is mine

I find it good

and greet each hour with gratitude.

We've been constrained, too much, too long
And now we've left our cage…!"

From a song by Lynne Heraud,
'The Working Man'

The Beginning

I have to write my story down because it's too horrendous and upsetting for me to say out loud.

It's too hurtful, painful and brings back too many awful memories for me to be able to talk about, after being forced to keep it quiet for a lifetime, but I want to record it so that my family and friends can understand.

Also, it should ensure that nothing similar happens to any of my grandchildren…

The occasional times that I have mentioned what my married life was like behind closed doors, both to family members and friends, have been met with silent, disbelieving stares—rather than the understanding and sympathy that I needed.

I have been divorced for well over four years now, and my ex-husband is still ringing me, calling at the place where I work and offering to do any odd jobs that I need doing.

He says that it's because he's sorry, and that he just wants to be near me, but I know that it's because he can't stand his own company, and longs to be back in the fold and security of a family, besides having a tame cook, cleaner and bottle washer…

He's also laid down rules about when I can visit my daughter and her family, which is another way of exercising control, ensuring that we don't meet there, but yet he wants us to meet in secret. Thus, he's still limiting the time I see my family, to suit his needs.

He believes that I can forgive him and forget what hell he put me through.

He is still unaware of the depth of harm he caused me, and thinks that I can forget all the dreadful memories he has given me over the years because he has 'behaved himself' (his words) since the divorce.

He's always been very, very careful to present an angelic appearance to the outside world.

A natural liar—he can talk his way out of any situation, regardless of the actual facts and makes an art out of being an extremely good actor.

For most of my married life I was swung between being frightened of him, and feeling sorry for him, because I knew from the beginning that he was sick in some way—I just didn't realise how deep rooted, strong and advanced the sickness was. I was very naïve and fondly thought that he would soon alter his ways if I turned the other cheek—and that he would respond to good treatment I was very young and foolish, with a head full of dreams...

Carleton Yorkshire

One of my earliest childhood memories—I suppose I'd be three or four years old—was of staying with my grandma, at her sister's house, at haymaking time. In those days, neighbouring farmers used to help each other on a rota basis to gather the hay for the forthcoming Winter, no big machinery to do it then, just lots of man power, baling twine and a couple of tractors and trailers.

My grandma used to help in the preparation of food— especially the bread baking—oh, I can remember the extremely seductive smell of the freshly baked bread! They churned their butter from their own cow's milk, so they knew exactly what had gone into the production of it. Hearty soups and large slices of crusty, buttered, bread still warm—whether by the summer heat or the oven, it still just kept the farmhouse, slightly salty butter, at melting point.

My memories of those days have stood me in good stead throughout my life, and made me realise how very important a happy childhood is.

That doesn't mean having all your own way, or being allowed to watch TV for hours on end whilst being fed regularly.

It's being treat fairly and made to feel valued and understood, having someone close in whom you can confide and trust, and being surrounded from time to time by good natured, like-minded people, whether family or friends who have a common aim or bond in which you can participate.

This hay making time fitted all those requirements, and I felt completely happy and satisfied.

My grandma had a stepsister, Belle, who lived at Carleton, a village near Skipton, Yorkshire with her husband who is a farmer, Bill Archer, and four children.

Belle was a kindly soul, always had a biscuit and drink for me, and a gentle, reassuring word. Her physique wasn't brilliant, she sort of hobbled around holding furniture, and I gathered from the dark whispers, that I overheard, that the hysterectomy after her fourth child had damaged her permanently.

It took me a long time to work out what 'everything taken away' meant!

In those days, work and money were sparse, and people had to make do and mend. Farmers didn't have much equipment—a tractor, scythes and rakes seemed to be all that was available, along with baling twine. It was sheer muscle power that determined the pace and rate of work, and farmers had to work from dusk till dawn more often than not, to keep the wolf from the door.

So, the local farmers all helped each other in turn with haymaking—a very community minded spirit, which just seemed to happen automatically.

This 'mucking in together' worked, and bonded them, the original support group—which saw them through the bad times and allowed them to enjoy, and share, the good occasions. Grandma went to live in for six weeks to help with the meals, bake bread, cakes, biscuits and cope with the extra housework and washing.

I remember them trying to make me go the village school, but I declined, much preferring the exciting haymaking and being with good people. There was always lots of good-natured talking, joking and shouting. They were determined to make it as much fun as possible.

I don't recall one word of dissention or negativity at all.

Uncle Bill and Aunt Belles' children were Jack, Harry, Jean and Sadie.

Jack was a young, keen, loyal air gunner and navigator in the RAF who was killed in action in the war.

One of my lasting memories is of Harry throwing me on to the 'roof' of a hay rick, landing me on my bottom, and when I slid down, unsuccessfully clutching at straws, breathlessly screaming with giddiness, he would catch me just in time, and throw me aloft again. Delightful. Heaven-high exhilaration, which has never been equalled in my life—so far!

The Bread Knife
and the Tie

Those young, happy, fresh, carefree, outdoor days at Carleton have obviously left a lasting impression on me!

Another incident that lay dormant in my head for a long lot of years, that I now recall, is of the men coming in from a very, long, hot, tiring, 'top of summer' day. They were all weary and overheated, through wearing what we'd think were the wrong clothes today. Instead of jeans and t-shirts, they just wore their old clothes that had automatically been handed down from being their 'best suit', to 'second best' then third, until they degenerated into working clothes.

Thus, they ended up wearing quite heavy 'serviceable' trousers and the long-sleeved shirts that had always gone with that particular set of apparel!

Far too heavy and thick for the extremely strenuous, labour intensive, sweaty job of haymaking in boiling, searing, sun drenched July and August.

The farmhouse doors and windows were all wide open, to let the air circulate.

It was alive and busy, with wives and daughters bustling around, setting the big table, arranging chairs, chatting, cooking, baking, bringing the washing in off the line, and generally contributing to keep the place clean and full of food and drink—they also made their own lemonade, ginger beer and nettle wine, incidentally!

They were short of nothing they had!

My particular memory cameo and time capsule is of watching Aunt Belle slicing a huge loaf of freshly baked, crusty bread, on a large, sturdy, well-scrubbed, wooden, chopping board.

She used an enormous, old, bone handled, knife that had a serrated blade, which had been sharpened on a whetstone so often that most of the serration had worn away.

She must have known that it would all be eaten at that meal because she had really swung into a rhythm of cutting it all up into regular slices.

I stood watching her fascinated, silently counting each number of regular, sawing strokes to the slice.

One of these hot, thirsty, hungry, neighbouring farmers, had an extra distressed look about him as he came up to the table, stood near to her and said, "This tie is nearly choking me, Belle. I can't get this bloody knot undone, and it's getting tighter…"

Without any comment, or breaking her carving rhythm, she smiled, gave a half turn to face him, took hold of his tie, raised her huge knife and sliced through the offensive article as though it was an everyday occurrence!

"God, what a relief. Thanks a million!" said the man, as he walked away to refresh himself prior to relaxing.

Aunt Belle smiled back at him—and me—then applied her knife back to the loaf as though nothing had happened…it just seemed humorously ordinary and right at the time, but I've never seen anyone do it since.

What faith that man must have had in her to unflinchingly handle such a sharp implement so near to his face and throat!

It must have been a rare, unique sight, a moment in history which has remained swirling around in the mists of my memory until now!

Carleton 2

They also kept hens, and I loved to 'help' Harry to feed them. One day, a small bird, probably a young sparrow or wren was in a hen hut, trying to escape. Harry said that he'd catch it for me. The poor bird must have been very frightened, for it was determined not to be caught.

It took Harry ages, and then when he had it in his huge hands, he walked outside, turned to me and said, "Here, this is for you."

I held my four years old hands out, and as I closed my fingers around the bird, it did what all little birds do, fluttered hard.

That was unexpected, and scared me.

I shouted and let it go, to watch it fly gratefully into the air—thankful and free…

Harry just laughed, picked me up and carried me back to the farmhouse.

I have very happy memories of Carleton, a shiny, copper bath, churning cream to make a salty butter, collecting eggs from under hens, (barbaric?), and going out in the pony and trap to deliver milk.

In those days, people left their milk jugs, and milk jug covers (small cotton/linen, lacy pieces of fabric, weighted down with beads) outside their houses, to be filled by the milkman from a big aluminium churn, by dipping and filling quart, pint or gill measures. Something that would make the EEC regulations do a Scottish reel, whilst standing on their heads!

Carrying armsfull of clean clothes in from the washing line, the swing that was just over the wall and the continual smell of cooking, the best of all was the magnetic aroma of newly baked bread. No supermarkets to spoil us for choice, just using the ingredients that were available, and every day practice at making the most of them.

Also, the sun always seemed to shine there, not like rainy Burnley, with its wet, shiny, cobbled streets.

My Mother
Dora Chatterton

My mother and her sister, Caroline—always shortened to Carrie—grew up in the village shop at Baxenden, near Accrington, which their parents—Albert and Margaret Chatterton owned and ran.

Fruit, vegetables and salad stuff were in good supply because my granddad had a fruit and vegetable stall on Accrington market.

He also ran a coal round, employing a man to do the manual work and deliveries!

She used to tell me that the shop sold anything and everything that was available in those days.

The stock would have been fairly limited by today's standards, but, for a corner shop, it amply supplied the villager's needs and provided a good living for the family.

Paraffin and firelighters were for sale there, along with bread, cakes, sticking plasters, shoe polish and laces, babies teething powders, Scot's emulsion, Fennings' fever curer, rat poison, mouse traps, tinned goods and drinks, sweets, ice-cream and all the other things that helped to make lives easier and better for people.

The EEC would probably have an apoplectic fit if they could see it now!

My mum told me that she and Carrie liked chocolate creams, peppermint and coffee flavoured in particular, and they must not have been so well defined as they are now.

So the two girls would sneak into the shop when it was closed, and stick a pin into the back of the chocolate creams. If it sank in, they knew that it was a soft centre, and probably a cream, but they'd reject the hard-centred caramels—replacing them in the box!

My mother was a hairdresser and a good swimmer. She enjoyed getting up early on Sunday mornings and going to the local pool in her little red sports car.

One such morning, it was frosty and as she touched her brakes, her car went into a spin and whisked her through the window of a town centre shop, smashing the glass.

Being horrified at what had happened, and no-one else to be seen anywhere, she drove back home, put her car away, and went back to bed.

Her mother said later that a policeman had called to ask about the incident, but Margaret declared indignantly that 'her daughter was safely tucked up in bed, and wouldn't be disturbed because she worked hard' so the policeman went away and nothing more was ever heard or said about the incident!

Harry Turner, My Father

Dora, my future mother, then met Harry Turner, who was to become my father.

They eventually married, living at Roughlee, a small village approximately twelve miles away from Burnley. The house that they bought was attached to a laundry, and whilst the laundry was running and working, their house had electricity supplied free from its' generator.

But, when the laundry closed for the weekend and every night, my mum and dad hadn't got any power!

So they didn't live there for very long, which was a shame because it's quite a pretty, unspoilt village even now, making every effort to resist change and retain its Olde Worlde Charme. Their next move was to Colne, where they purchased a detached, mock Tudor show home for the princely sum of £750!

This was 269 Burnley Road Colne where my brother, Derek Arthur, and I, Constance Margaret, were born in the front bedroom!

Six years apart—me being the younger.

My dad had got a business going—dealing in textiles, basically buying and selling, although he did build a very small dye works in which he attempted to dye and finished loom state cotton and artificial silk. He had a man running it for him, a retired dye worker by the name of Fred Speak, who just used to turn up one or two days a week.

But before that happy state of affairs came about, he was called up to do his stuff for the war effort.

He was put in the Eighth Army as a tank driver, and had to go to El Alamein, Cairo, Tobruck, Alexandria, etc., for the five or six years that it lasted, just returning home once because his neck became covered in boils. When he had recovered and just grown accustomed to family life again, he had to return to the war in the Middle East.

Winston Churchill was convinced that the battle of El Alamein marked the turning point in the war and ordered the ringing of church bells all over Britain. As he said later:

Before Alamein, we never had a victory, after Alamein, we never had a defeat.

Montgomery and the Eighth Army continued to move forward and captured Tripoli on 23rd January 1943. Rommel was unable to mount a successful counterattack

Our English soldiers held Field Marshall Montgomery in high esteem, and the eighth army, whose emblem was 'Fear Naught', became known as Rommel's Desert Rats—it sounds awful now, but it evidently had some sort of prestige in those days, and our boys were quite proud to have made their mark in this way!

He recounted many stories to my brother and I of all the trials and tribulations that happened—including witnessing many of his close friends being killed…bathing in petrol because of the water shortages, bodies being robbed by British soldiers, hands and fingers of bodies being cut off to remove watches and rings, pages of the Bible manufactured from rice paper were torn out to make roll up cigarettes, flame throwers used to set fire to people and burn them—whether dead or alive, so many horrific memories that today would be worthy of compensation from the government, but in those days, after the war, those men and women just had to return and pick up the threads of normality as best they could.

There are never any winners in war…

My mother, meanwhile, had been running the business to the best of her ability, but it was forced medicine and she didn't cope perfectly with it.

She became used to having a few friends in on a fairly regular basis, initially to help, and this led to a few drinks being taken as a means of relaxation.

Eventually, the drink became a habit that she couldn't control, and so she developed into an alcoholic.

Growing up with an alcoholic mother is not easy.

You soon learn that it is a dreadful secret that your friends wont/can't understand, and it's also too painful to admit even to yourself.

I well remember once running in the house, excitedly bringing a newly made friend to show off the house to her and introduce her to my family.

I ran in through the kitchen into the dining room, shouting that I was home and to my abject horror, my mother was so full of alcohol that she was out cold on the settee, quite dead to the world, impervious to her surroundings, and smelling of drink.

I then had to think very quickly of an excuse to get my new friend away before she saw and began to guess the truth.

We never knew what state she'd be in when we came home. When she was sober, she was a wonderful mother, running the house and kitchen according to Mrs Beeton.

But when she was drunk, she was completely unmanageable, impractical and degraded.

My dad was quite at a loss as to how to stop her. He also liked a drink, very rarely to excess, but he too enjoyed entertaining, and there was always a good selection of beers, wines, spirits and liqueurs in the house.

He often despaired, but was fiercely loyal, and could never bring himself to get angry with her. And so, the situation was tolerated, as it grew worse and more intense, finally resolving itself in her death from liver failure.

On the morning that she was to pass away, we knew that the end was near. The doctor called regularly by now and I just about knew that I was pregnant with my second baby.

I tried to tell her that a new, vibrant life was on the way, but she was drifting in and out of a coma.

However, as I told her for the third time, she opened her eyes really wide and nodded.

Thus, I felt that my message had got through to her, however momentarily...

My baby girl was born almost seven months to the day later.

Addiction

During this time, or earlier now that I've thought about it, when I was nine, ten or eleven, I used to wonder why my mother went 'funny' at night.

My dad wouldn't comment, and I eventually realised that she was drunk.

Alcoholism affects every member of the family and makes life difficult for all concerned.

It's like having an elephant in the room, but no one is allowed to acknowledge its presence!

Simple things like school plays, open evenings where parents could attend or buying new uniform items, became a worry for me, in case anyone guessed the dark secret.

She never did let me down on these occasions, but they were still anxious times for me.

When she was sober, she was a brilliant person. We had a 'daily' and Mother used to cook proper meals, no cutting expenses or corners—no ready-mades or frozen meals in those days—we had proper cutlery—fish knives for fish, linen tablecloths and napkins with rings, etc., always fresh flowers and the niceties of life, but when she decided to let go—boy, she went!

Evidently, it started during the war, when my dad was away and she invited friends round for company and help.

They in turn, brought drink and food (rationing applied at this time), and so the pattern began.

She developed a liking for alcohol, which became a habit—a dependence crutch and she couldn't stop.

My dad was in a quandary about it.

A family friend, Dr Forbes, used to advise stopping her money, then she couldn't buy it or pay someone to bring it in for her.

At the same time, my dad liked to drink—the habit grew stronger after the war had changed their lives. Often, my cousins, John and David were brought by their parents, Uncle Arthur and Auntie Lily, and as they like to drink, out would come the booze.

We children could play as and how we liked, we had to supervise ourselves, and with no TV to watch, we made our own games.

John and I were always compatible and enjoyed being silly—whereas his brother, David, was more for sitting with a book, and didn't want to be disturbed.

Our house had a spiral staircase with one complete turn, and it and the hall were wood panelled which meant we didn't have to guard against dirtying the wallpaper! Indoor sledging was one riotous game that we devised.

This was when we both sat on the same tray together and spiralled, slid, bumped and banged all the way down the stairs, hanging on for dear life, screaming and shouting all the while!

Much better than TV and an ideal way to let off steam…all children should be allowed to do that, if only a few times in their life!

Times were not at all bad, and I have lots of happy memories, which have stood me in good stead throughout the years

So, there was always alcohol in the house, lots of people—customers and friends to entertain, and plenty of spare money to top it up.

Derek and I were quite helpless to alter, resolve or mend the situation.

All we could do was watch her slowly deteriorate and hope that she would see sense one day.

Tippler Toilet

Until things returned to normal, I lived a lot of the time with my paternal grandmother, Mary Ada (Turner) nee Mitton.

Her stone-built house, 30 Woodbine Road Burnley, was a three-bedroomed terraced, probably built around 1900. It had an out kitchen, with the bathroom on top of it, living room, front parlour, which was only used when visitors came (if they warranted it, Christmas, and high days), a lobby and vestibule. It's most memorable feature for me was the toilet. It was housed in the air raid shelter, along with a dolly tub and posser, old mangle and several storage items.

She never called it anything else but the 'air raid shelter'.

Built in the back garden, this 'air raid shelter' housed this unique toilet.

It was a square, brick-built block (which was white-washed every year) with a hole in it, topped by a wooden seat, that met your eyes, and commanded your attention.

If you dared to look down the hole, searching for the bottom, you could feel your eyes extending and stretching into the velvety blackness—as though staring down a bottomless pit.

My brother, Derek, once dropped a bottle of Haworths sarsaparilla down to see what happened, and judge its' depth, by listening and timing how long it took to land!

Boy, oh boy—was he in trouble for that!

It was a tippler toilet which as far as I know, gathered the rainwater from the roof's troughing and piped it underground to flush with—as the unseen bucket filled with water, it overbalanced and spilled its contents—washing the whole lot into the underground drain several feet below, which carried its cargo on its merry way.

A marvellous piece of Victorian ingenuity and slightly Heath Robinson-ish!

On a rainy day, which was very frequent in Burnley, and when there was a good heavy downpour—the tippler was forever flushing whether it needed to do or not!

She was an independent character, probably because she had three sons, and her husband had died of a heart attack when he was 49 years old.

I don't think there would be much help from social security so long ago, and she worked as a weaver in the local mill—her husband was a tackler who kept the looms running.

She told me that she began work at six o'clock in the morning, and then she got a break at eight o'clock. At that time, she used to run up the road, get her three sons up, washed, dressed and breakfasted and off to school, then she had to run back to the mill to begin her work there again

The same routine at lunchtime—home to feed the boys, get them back to school, before running down the road to the mill to continue the weaving!

As soon as her shift was over at tea time, she had to speed home, to look after her family, finding time to listen to them about their school life, coping with cooking, cleaning, shopping and laundry single-handedly.

These days, we don't know we're born!

Horses

She had a love of horses, not to ride them but to bet on them!

Before bookies became legal off course, or away from racecourses, there used to be men that would hang round public places and had regular haunts, to collect money and bets from people that couldn't get to a racecourse.

They were known as bookies runners, and my grandma used to have one of these men call at her house on a given day. She'd have studied form from the newspaper, most likely the *News Chronicle*, chosen her 'winner', written her bet on a piece of paper, placed money in it (probably a shilling each way…), twisted or folded the paper round the money, and off he'd trot with it to his boss, the Bookmaker.

The love of horses runs through my family like a vein. My uncle Arthur—my father's brother—kept and bred horses in Yorkshire for as long as I remember, having many winners and lots of losers. But he was always convinced that he would breed a world-beater one day, and never gave up hope.

One of the horses that he bred was a mare named Snow Blossom, whom he sold. She then gave birth to a horse called Snow Knight who won the English Derby in 1974.

Snow Knight went to the States after his Derby win. In 1975, he was named Champion American grass horse and was awarded an eclipse award.

Uncle Arthur died before this prestigious event, so, sadly, he never knew his greatest triumph.

His son, John, lives in California with his wife, Carol and daughter, Lucy, and has stuck to the same idea, much the same principle.

He has made a good name for himself and he lives very well on it.

Uncle Arthur decided years ago that he would trace the family tree, long before it became fashionable to do so.

He hired a man to do it for him for it was a laborious job then, no internet, just slogging around churches, graveyards and record offices.

After this man had spent some time and money in this pursuit, one of the gems he came up with was that one of our ancestors was hung for stealing a horse!

So Uncle Arthur called off the search at that point!

Both my daughters rode as children and young adults, Carolyn still does. She and her husband, Barry, have Rayne Riding Centre, in Essex, and her daughter is as keen as anyone on horses and horse riding.

So it must be in the blood!

Burnley

Back in Burnley, I remember vividly my first day at Lionel Street School.

My teacher was Miss Rice—she had a round, kind face and curly, black hair.

There were no pre-schools or nurseries then, not for us anyway, so it was quite a jump, to have four years of security at home, in familiar surroundings, then start full time school.

I remember wondering why so many of the children were crying in this new, exciting place…it all looked so good to me. The only recollection of the war that I have is when some woman tried to put a Mickey Mouse gas mask on me and I thought she was trying to suffocate me.

My dad said, "If she doesn't want it on, leave it off!" My saviour!

Grandma told me that she was once wakened in the middle of the night by a patrolling warden hammering at the door, who could see a chink of light shining through the blackout curtains that hadn't been drawn exactly together.

She'd gone to bed, forgetting to put the light out—leaving a clue to passing enemy aircraft that the area was inhabited, thus encouraging them to drop a bomb! She was warned that if ever she did it again, she'd 'get a summons next time!'.

All in all, a happy time, visiting my father's brothers house. Uncle Arthur—a large detached, and playing with my cousins, John and David.

They had a grand piano, which no one ever played, and my cousins used to push coins between the keys for a game!

A large Ingle Nook fireplace, all out of carved wood that incorporated a small seat at each side of the hearth.

His settee was always full of Horse Breeders magazines—his dream was to breed the perfect horse that could win every prize it entered for.

Alas, it remained a dream, but his son, John, inherited the love of horses and made money from it, so I'm sure Uncle Arthur would be tickled pink if he knew!

Taking flowers to the cemetery with my grandma—and putting them on Grandads grave—picking blackberries 'on't back o't trap' and 'helping my grandma to make blackberry jelly from them.

Eating this jelly in winter always brought back the memories of picking them on a hot summer day—so they served two purposes.

Then my parents must have felt that they had got the business back on track, so I went back to live permanently with them and my brother.

Just After the War

Just after the war, life took some time to return to normal.

Lots of the men had been away for five or six years, experiencing all the horrors of war, and upon return, were expected to carry on as they did before, as though nothing had happened.

I'm not sure if this occurred in any other part of the world, but, where I lived in the north of England, I well remember the sound of small wheels on the 'flagged' pavement.

This was a homemade vehicle, and consisted of a small, wooden, square board with a wheel attached to each corner, upon which sat a man.

This man was legless and he used to propel himself along by means of a small piece of wood, wrapped in fabric, for silence and better grip I suppose.

There were two of these men, each in a different part of town, and I think that they were war victims. The story was that they'd had their legs blown off in battle.

I used to think that they could go quite fast for their ages, but, upon reflection, I guess they wouldn't be that old—thirty or forty at most.

No special compensation or lavish payments like they'd get if it happened now.

No outcry or special treatment, they just accepted it and got on with their lives as best they could.

We children used to gaze in wonderment as they rowed their way about the pavements and roads, not really understanding the true horror therein.

Talk about every picture tells a story!

But all these memories of being away from home in strange countries, confusing languages and customs, watching explosions, shootings, lootings, deprivation and, often, having seen their friends die in combat, altered their way of thinking, acting and feeling for the rest of their lives.

In England, food, sweets, clothing and petrol had been rationed; only a set amount per person per week, and these were allocated by means of rationing coupons.

A black market existed, whereby certain goods were obtainable amongst the people in the know, but it was against the law.

Ironically, the nation's health improved with these food shortages, maybe there's a lesson to be learned…

My dad had a farmer friend/neighbour who kept pigs. From him, my dad bought 'some hams'—full legs of pork.

These he hung in the garage, which had had the windows blacked out, and we were all sworn to secrecy about them, cos the amount of meat per person on ration, was meagre. The allowance was something like eight oz. or four oz. per person per week.

Such was the tight regulation on coupons.

Derek and I used these full ham shanks for dartboard practice!

My dad knew and didn't care.

There was something exciting and satisfying about sinking a dart into the flesh—and the knowledge that there would be ham and eggs for some time to come! When the war finished, and factories gradually picked up the reins of business and distribution. The shops suddenly became exciting places, becoming stocked with food and all sorts of delights.

Spearmint chews; sherbet lemons, milkmaid caramels, all sorts of delights became slowly available, and were received with grateful thanks!

My school was Primet Secondary Modern, about half a mile away from my home. My Elswick Hopper bicycle used to get me there in a few minutes, so I never stayed to school dinners—for which I was always glad. I used to hear awful reports about them from my classmates.

I took the eleven plus twice, and failed it twice.

At the first failure, my teachers were very upset, and they insisted that I retry.

By then, I was having such a good time at this almost brand-new school with all mod cons—science laboratory, woodwork room, domestic science room, gymnasium with showers, male and female—all fully equipped and bang up to date. It was light and airy, with lots of big windows and heating that worked properly—unlike many other antiquated buildings in the area.

A Huge Hall

The school was very new and it housed a huge hall that we could use freely on wet days for dancing and other activities.

As the area was hilly, the clouds lingered and lodged there, causing the rain to fall on more days than not, so we danced for the latter part of most of the lunch breaks!

There were two young PE teachers, Eric Proctor and Margaret Foulds, that we thought were brilliant.

They allowed us to do all sorts of stuff, and I soon learnt to quick step and 'bop' down the wide, straight corridors with the older girls, and as I was always good at English. The English teacher, Frank Bannister, put on drama productions and I was always included somehow.

At the second try, I knew I didn't want to leave and so I just sat around during the exam, leaving my papers incomplete. What I later learnt was, at that time, only a percentage of bright girls were allowed into Grammar schools, whereas if any boys showed an academic aptitude, they were accepted into higher education.

This was why the teachers were so angry at the unfairness of the system.

My brother went to Colne Grammar School which was about five miles away by road, or two miles the 'fields' way. He got lots of homework and pressure, whereas I got hardly any.

So I was glad not to be pushed so hard.

He ended by getting his exams, and playing cricket and rugby for Nelson and Colne, gaining several caps along the way by playing for Lancashire.

Then, when he was 18, he had to do his national service for two years, along with every other able-bodied boy. He was posted to Leyland, in the Fylde, where he qualified as a motorbike mechanic.

So, he emerged, after two years in the RAF with a career. My dad just wanted me to work for him in the family textile business and I knew that the money was good, even though there weren't any prospects.

But, when I was a young teenager, I didn't care!

So I was never encouraged to pass exams, and university was never mentioned—even discouraged

I was just expected to be in the family business, which was standing markets, helping load and unload vans, and watching the hard-earned money being spent, rather than used properly—like buying buildings made from bricks and mortar, which would make a profit one day. I always used to begrudge watching the money handed over for market rents, and just frittered away, instead of saving for the future.

So did Derek.

But we knew he wouldn't change, and if we stayed put, there was always a good lifestyle as long as we stayed in father's care.

Those gossamer strands that tie families together are invisible, but can hardly ever be broken, apart from in exceptional circumstances.

He actually taught me quite a lot about life just by being in a close family business.

We had quite a few Jewish customers, who had Saturday as their Sabbath, and were used to working on Sundays.

When they came on these days, my dad would often call me to go in the room and talk to them whilst he went on to the warehouse.

I wasn't very old—ten, eleven or twelve and didn't know how to talk to strangers, let alone entertain them.

I remember refusing to do it, saying, "I don't know what to say!"

But my dad would respond, "I don't care what you talk about—read from a newspaper, describe your dress, what you do at school, the weather, anything! If they're left to their own devices, they'll go through drawers, invoices etc., find out how much I've paid for the cloth, and won't pay the price I'm asking them to pay.

"Furthermore, if you don't go in and keep them talking, you won't get your spending money this week!"

So, I would face these customers—often a different lot each week and I very soon learnt that the easiest way was for me to ask them questions.

When once they relaxed and began talking about themselves, I knew that I was home and dry.

I actually began to enjoy listening to all the varied tales that they told, each one demonstrating a snippet of their different customs, religions and lifestyles.

It taught me a lot about people, and I have never been scared to talk to strangers since because I know that we all have our story to tell...

When my daughters had grown up, I did a counselling course, and I realised that this was what I subconsciously learned to do early on in life

My dad was ahead of his time...

My First Driving Lesson

My dad couldn't wait to get me out and about, driving and carrying textiles around, he gave me my first driving lesson in France when I was fifteen years old!

This was on a disused runway that we happened across in France when we were on holiday.

It was ideal for learning to drive, just a huge expanse of concrete without any traffic lights, zebra crossings or suchlike!

He soon had me driving up and down, carefully explaining the rudiments of driving and allowing me to gradually get used to the steering, gears and brakes.

Then, he said he'd test me!

He got out, stood by the side of the tarmac/concrete, and suggested that I take the car, by myself, up the runway and back and see if I could stop right by him so that he could just open the door and get in!

Which I did, with all the confidence of a young teenager!

It must have done me good because I passed my driving test first time, despite exceeding the speed limit!

I value the freedom and coolness of that lesson much more now, because I just took it for granted at the time!

Those silken ties that bind are very strong indeed.

I Loved Dancing

I loved dancing—I'd had piano, tap and ballet lessons, but stopped when my teacher told me I'd never be tall enough to be a professional dancer!

When I was fourteen or fifteen, I used to go down Albert Street. This was a large first floor room where we could buy soft drinks, crisps and play records. Anyone could sing if they'd a mind to, using the mike, and we learnt to jive or 'bop' as well as the quickstep. They played the modern music of the day—Elvis was king there and very exciting. My mother wouldn't allow an Elvis record in the house—gyrating hips were bad for us!

So Albert Street was a source of delight to me, freedom to do more or less whatever we liked—I'm sure there must have been an adult there, but I have no recollection of restriction in any sense or form.

Then, we progressed down the 'Imp'.

The Imperial ballroom was a large, modern ballroom, that attracted all the big bands of the day, Ted Heath, Johnny Dankworth, Ray Ellington, even the Beatles were scheduled to appear there, but they rapidly became too popular for small Nelson—being mobbed wherever they went, so they had to cancel their engagement.

I didn't tell my parents about my visits there. They would have considered it too old for me, so I used to go there on Saturday nights, after I'd stood Oldham's Tommyfield market with my dad.

I took a vanity case with my grown-up stuff in, and stayed with a friend overnight.

That's where I met Roy Redmayne.

He took me home on the bus once or twice, and seemed very nice. He was an electrician, and, as we began to see more and more of each other, I began to think that being an electrician's wife would simplify things, and I'd be away from my father, who, although good as gold to me, didn't want to lose me, especially as he could see that he was losing his wife—my mother—to drink.

I wanted to be a hairdresser, but my dad said I'd only have to wash heads and sweep up, thus dismissing my suggestion.

When I was in my very early teens, he also told me that when I was old enough, he'd find the right boy for me—I'd a feeling that he already had some mill owner's son lined up for me, and I dreaded the thought!

I knew then that I had to make my own decision as to my future—but when you're aged fourteen, it's difficult, if not impossible, to see the big picture and understand how the world works.

I began to want to spread my wings and my dad knew that I was ready to leave his world, although I'd no idea how to go about it, because I'd been too sheltered…a bird in a golden cage…

Some Buys Were
Not All Good!

My dad was the original 'Del boy', but as successful as he needed or wanted to be.

He didn't have dreams of building an empire, he just wanted to give his family a good time whilst it lasted.

His mainstay for making money was converting loom state fabric into bleached, dyed and finished materials, then selling it.

He was good at the game, and knew the trade inside out by keeping up to date with current trends. This enabled him to convince his peers that this particular purchase was bang up to date and would be a profitable buy.

But, as a side line, he was always on the lookout for anything that was cheap and could be sold for a good profit.

As a consequence, lots of escapades happened, one of which was when a mill that he dealt with was experimenting with elastin, the forerunner of Lycra. The fabric looked good, a heavy satin that stretched, and people bought it and made figure hugging, swimsuits that fitted beautifully from it.

What we didn't know was that when the fabric became wet, it relaxed and stretched, never to regain its elasticity!

We had reports, called feedback these days, of people coming out of the sea, hauling and dragging their heavy, waterlogged swimsuits behind them with one hand, and trying to cover their embarrassment with the other!

Another buy that I remember was a mixed lot of between four and five hundred umbrellas—a rack full.

The gents' ones were plain black or navy, and the ladies' ones were all shades and designs—very varied, striped, floral, polka dot, plain pastels, bright colours and all looked very attractive.

They sold well for very little money and proved quite popular in our damp, rainy area.

Then, we gradually began to get reports about this stock, and it seemed that approximately two thirds of them were very good quality, and did the job well that they were designed to do.

But the other third was not so good because when once they were put up, love, money or brute force wouldn't persuade them to come back down!

Those ones had to be thrown away!

When dad's customers had a valid complaint about their purchase, he always refunded their money cheerfully and without question.

The uncertain stock that he sold, without any comeback at all, gave him much satisfaction, pleasure and glee!

He knew how to extract fun out of any situation, and would always exaggerate the humour to make a very tell-able story.

Pre-Decimalisation

He was willing to give me anything to keep me close and at home. It was always unspoken, but I was beginning to feel just like a special, experimental animal in a good, open, spacious cage, everything I needed, quite secure in my surroundings, but never quite free.

He knew that I wasn't happy working for him and that I wanted the independence and freedom of a job somewhere.

University would have fitted the bill perfectly, but he got me a job at Proctor and Proctors, his accountants!

No calculators in those days, my dad had a huge Burroughs adding machine. A big, metal monster, that stood on four legs.

It was made from iron, far too heavy to lift, so it was on castors!

A museum piece when he bought it—a total curiosity, a practical, talking point!

My dad got a job for me at his accountants, knowing that I wouldn't last too long there and he must have silently hoped that I would be glad to go back to the comparative security of working with him.

Working at Proctor & Proctor, the accountants and auditors was quite exciting for me at first.

It was my first step into the real world, amongst real people, doing a real job, and I was going to try to make a good, successful job of it.

In the beginning, I was on the telephone linking system. I had to accept incoming calls and redirect them to the appropriate office, as well as fetch and carry, and make tea!

This was pre-decimalisation, so, as an apprentice, I graduated to adding up long columns of figures up in pounds, shillings and pence!

God, how I hated it!

But then, we went out on audits, which I enjoyed because it entailed visiting the local businesses and meeting the staff therein.

My young way of thinking was no more than having my own little house, a husband that would love me forever and adorable children that would make our happy lives complete.

I loved fiction/mythology/fairy stories and dreamt of living inside one.

The first boy that walked into my life had an entirely different set of ideas—a very hidden agenda—which I was to hear about sooner than I realised!

Suspenders and Stockings

Seventeen years old, at a time when girls still had to conform to the standards of the day, and wondering which road to take.

University was never, ever considered for me, even though my parents could easily have financially afforded to let me go—I think my father found it difficult to emotionally let me go, and was secretly glad when I didn't pass my scholarship because then I wouldn't get any high-flown ideas about leaving home to become independent, which, looking back, was what I really wanted—and needed.

So, I made the decision to jump off, maybe get myself pregnant, which was partly what 'fashionable' at the time—before the pill was in general usage, and the boys were too macho to want to bother using condoms.

Then I met a handsome, young electrician and I saw my way out of textiles.

Roy seemed fairly lively, and fun loving on limited means. I was young (16) when I met him and thought that I could make him happy as an electrician's wife and have a somewhat normal life myself, as opposed to my parent's wild side, merry go round lifestyle.

He cottoned onto the idea very quickly, and was only too keen to do it anytime, anywhere.

Even once on top of a bus between Nelson and Colne!

I suppose it wasn't too difficult, me in a tight, black skirt with a split, stockings held up by a suspender belt, no awkward tights to have to struggle and fight with!

The favourite place was my house on a Saturday afternoon. I'd told my dad that if I was now working at

Proctor and Proctor, the accountants—I shouldn't have to go to market with him on Saturdays. That left the house free for me—and I invited Roy along to tea—salmon sandwiches etc., and he'd bring along his Mario Lanza LP of the Student Prince.

I always thought that Mario was a bit manic; it's funny what you see with hindsight because that's how Roy turned out to be—they were like-minded individuals.

I saw more of Roy, and yes, you've guessed it, became pregnant at the tender age of 17+three-quarters!

Harry Turner 2

When my mother died, my dad was devastated and didn't know where to put himself, or what to do for the best.

He threw himself into working harder than ever.

It was as if he had to fill in his time with activities in case another thought of her once again took over all his being.

He went on lots of holidays and several of these were with my Auntie Carrie (Mum's sister) and her husband, Billie.

Once, when they were in the heart of Paris, my dad went into an expensive florist's shop, bought a large, celebratory bouquet of red roses, made the ticket out 'With all my love to Dora' (my mother), walked to Pont Alexander, took a few moments to think of her, then he let it drop into the Seine in her memory, and stood watching it until it slowly drifted out of sight...

He also dropped her wedding ring into the river at the same time, so that no one else could ever wear it...

Romantic or what?

In contrast, I went to Paris with my husband for our 25th wedding anniversary for a few days.

Paris is always good, so I managed to enjoy it, despite the company eternally fault finding.

One day, we climbed the steps to the top of the Arc de Triumph, and stood admiring the views from up there.

He made a remark about 'the big building over there' and I said, "Which big building?" as there were plenty to be seen and I had been looking elsewhere.

His answer was, "Oh, you f–cking tw–t!" As he walked away from me, thus ruining what was meant to be a perfectly good city break holiday in a classy hotel!

Years later, after the divorce, I went on a romantic weekend to Paris with Lewis, of whom more later. We travelled by Eurostar and stayed at a smallish, fun hotel, that had been recently refurbished to hint at the style of Montmartre's red light area—our bedroom was named Brigitte Bardot, it had red, lace curtains at the balcony windows, the walls of our bedroom were lined with heavy, pink, moiré taffeta and even the television set was red and black!

We wandered at will round the city, did all the things that tourists enjoy doing, viewed Notre Dame and Sacre Coeur, saw the sights from the top of a tour bus, went to the top of the Eiffel tower, enjoyed a boat ride on the Seine, walked through the parks, ate and drank at pavement cafes—there was no dissention or negativity at all, and Paris was as beautiful as she always is…

Thus, restoring my faith in humanity

The Boyfriend

I met Roy's parents; they were just ordinary, quiet people. His mother was definitely the one in charge because I noticed very quickly, that as soon as his father began to speak, she would butt in and either tell him that he was wrong, or she'd finish his sentence for him—how she thought it should be said, completely disregarding his feelings,

Thus, making him appear foolish.

But he was the one that worked to keep the wolf from the door, whereas his mother just worked when she decided to earn some money for herself.

It wasn't until twenty years later when he used to do some gardening for us at Stocks house, Gisburn, that I heard him complete a sentence!

Because I listened to him and encouraged him to talk, he told me things about his family that my husband had never heard.

But Roy enjoyed the sound of his own voice much more than anyone else's, so that didn't surprise me at all!

I use to bring my father-in-law to our house, and he was a totally different person when he was by himself and relaxed…

Roy said that when he was young, his mother used to push him against the wall hard for punishment, bang his head on the wall, and shut him in the completely dark pantry, as methods of control.

He evidently showed signs of disturbance early on because he was expelled from nursery school for being disruptive and destructive. These two qualities have stayed with him, so I think they are in the genes.

Many years later, he had to leave Edge End School for the same reasons.

This was told to me when once we were married—if I'd learnt it earlier, I may have thought twice about going out with him, or been sensible enough to wait until the right boy came along!

The Wedding Was Weird

The wedding was weird.

It was on a Thursday—my dads' day off!

The Church was St Johns, Barkerhouse Road, Nelson. The vicar was Rev Morgan, who was aged about 90 and still able to terrify the local populace by driving around in his old, racing-green, open-topped Morgan sports car!

My dad managed to slip him a tenner and a bottle of whiskey whilst the register was being signed, which the reverend gratefully, carefully and promptly placed quietly in his desk drawer!

The reception was at Stirk House Hotel, Gisburn—quite a posh place in those days.

It was a large Yorkshire stone house, that had just recently been converted from a private dwelling into a hotel, so everything was brand-spanking-new, and of the highest quality. There were nine of us present; my mother and dad, Roy's mum and dad, my brother, Derek, and his wife, and my grandma, Roy and me.

My grandmother cried all the time—every time she looked at me, she just sobbed!

She'd already told me that I was throwing my life away—as had friends of my mother and dad—but I was young, optimistic and quite confident that I could make the marriage work.

Little did I know!

My grandma cried all through the meal—using about ten, large gents hankies!

My brother, Derek, took us to the station, where we caught a train for our four-day honeymoon.

My dad paid for us to go to London for four days at the Load of Hay Hotel, Praed St.

We moved into a little four-roomed house, 17 Reedyford Road, that my dad had bought from one of his friends who had been renting it out.

He also helped us to 'modernise' it, by paying for a new back drain, furniture and decorating, etc.

Roy rewired it with me helping as labourer, my dad had his plumber Alan Dent, dig up the back yard, and install new drains and a flush toilet there, also fitting a hot water geyser.

He also paid for us to have the main two rooms professionally decorated.

My grandma gave us money for a new bedroom suite; various friends of my parents and relations of mine gave us lots of necessities—towel, sheets, crockery etc.

I made the curtains, using my dad's fabric. He gave us their leather three-piece suite, paid for carpets, even their oak fireplace surround, replacing theirs with a rustic tiled affair.

Such was my father's love for me.

I loved it, and fondly imagined that this would be the start of a genuine, life-long union.

Friends of my family had been generous, and given us presents, and one of these was an antique, wooden, chiming clock of my grandmas' that kept excellent time, that she knew I liked.

He didn't like the chimes but they were only there if we wanted them to be because they had an on/off lever.

I felt affection for it because I knew that my grandma had cherished it for years.

It was bought for her by one of her sons, so it had more than its intrinsic value, it had sentimental value too…

One day, I was surprised to return home to discover that Roy had put this clock in the dustbin; just before the bin men collected it!

I didn't get too upset, it was only a clock, but it was my grandmas, and I liked it, so it was hurtful and I never forgot it…

He was still working as an electrician, and was becoming more distant—causing arguments over nothing, walking out and slamming the door behind him.

I'd never seen behaviour like that. One day, he surprised me even more.

I remember that he stood with his back to the window and said, "Do you know that the police won't come out to a call for domestic violence?"

I had never heard of domestic violence, too naïve to know what it meant, and when I found out, I was horrified, and wondered what, if anything, would happen because I also discovered that he was correct. Police used to ignore domestic violence, dismissing it as a 'lovers tiff'.

There were no Womens Refuges that I heard of, no benefits or accommodation for single mothers and going back to my Dad and Mum wasn't the answer, because they needed workers who weren't slowed down by children, besides, they were usually full of alcohol by night!

I didn't believe that Roy would be party to such behaviour…I was so wrong…

He was always good and well-mannered to me out amongst other people, and everyone thought he was wonderful, but, when once the door closed, he became so different, belligerent, sulky and beginning to threaten.

It was very difficult for me to understand because I had never come up against these 'mind games' that are played for a type of sadistic pleasure.

If he could reduce me to tears, he thought that he'd won, so would then become an earnest apologiser.

He told me that he would be all right with me in front of other people, and he was. Just as his mother was with his father…

All in all, we were very soon well set up, albeit in a small way, but we already had as much, if not more than, Roy's parents…

What he brought into the wedding home was a single wardrobe, his clothes and a sink plunger!

His mother said that he was good at unblocking the sink when she blocked it up with food…

So his contribution didn't amount to much at all, and I didn't care because until we were married, he was very caring, loving and appeared to like me very much.

Which was all that I wanted and expected.

I simply wanted a quiet, orderly, family life and I thought that was what I was getting.

Whereas, he just saw me as a meal ticket, so he never attempted to repay me in any way…

But he fed his inborn, selfish, callous instinct by abusing me, and making me feel inadequate by threatening, bellowing in my ear, throwing things across the room, slamming doors, sulking for days on end, scaring me into locking myself in the bathroom until he calmed down and generally giving vent to his many and varied tantrums.

He knew very well that I wanted to prove to everyone that I wasn't too young to marry, after all, and this would have a happy ending, come hell or high water…

I'd no idea just how determined he was to have all his own way, completely regardless of my feelings.

He Never Once Gave
Me a Witness

He never once gave me a witness to his other, secret, black side that he'd inherited from his mother.

Both times when I was pregnant, he pulled me downstairs by my ankles and laughed, saying it was, "Just for fun!"

If I'd had a miscarriage, he'd have completely denied any involvement, saying that I'd tripped and fallen.

Explaining to a questioner that I'd slipped accidentally, thus, in the eyes of the world, absolving himself from all blame.

Luckily, I managed to hang on to the babies, but I didn't get much fun out of being bumped down the stairs on my tummy!

I realised that as he was an only child, he was already jealous of the new life that was going to join us soon…

He was always sorry afterwards, and I fell into the trap of giving him sympathy because I knew that he had some sickness which I fondly imagined I could make better!

I didn't realise just how solid a hold the sickness had, or I wouldn't have believed that I could cure it by 'turning the other cheek', bouncing back as though nothing had happened, and keeping all his badness locked away inside me, so that no-one knew.

Pretending to the outside world that the marriage was good.

Looking back, I can see so clearly now how futile my endeavours were…

Everything he did to hurt me was always cleverly concealed, and could always be explained as though I'd had an accident pushing me against a wall, following me around the house, bellowing in my ear and making false accusations against me, making me feel guilty as though his appalling behaviour was brought on by me.

He could always find a way to show me that it was my fault!

I was young, supple, determined, resilient and full of hope that he would change one day. "Ha, ha," said the clown!

When our first daughter was born, my supply of breast milk was good.

I had too much for the baby, so the nurses showed me how to express it and it was given to any baby whose mothers milk supply was lacking. It was very creamy, and they told me that I could have sold it for top money, which made me feel that I was on the right track to being a good mother!

However, within a day or two of me taking the baby home, he made me stop breast feeding, saying that his mother wouldn't like it…

So, like a good wife, I bought bottles and some Cow & Gate dried milk, sterilising equipment and all the other paraphernalia that breast-feeding eliminates

Our second baby never even got the benefit of the first protective breast milk that is so advantageous to a new-born baby—as well as the bonding process between mother and child.

I gave in yet again, due to my reluctance to have yet another row.

He was very energetic, always on the go and hyperactive, providing he did what he wanted to do, and not have to work too hard for anyone else!

Very excitable, often good fun, but unstable, likely to 'fly off the handle' at the drop of a hat if events didn't go just as he had planned or as he wanted them to be. He was exceedingly garrulous, loving the sound of his own voice, and any silence had to be filled with it—no matter what he chattered about, the subject was irrelevant, it was the sound of him talking that was important.

He used to interrupt me on the third word of a sentence, just as his mother had done with his dad, using this as a method of control which was his favourite game.

I can also verify that there is such a thing as rape within marriage...

This irrational, illogical, volatile behaviour grew wearying in time and I just wanted peace, quiet and to have my own thoughts to myself.

When I was finally divorced, it was as though a huge weight had been lifted from my shoulders, and I had total freedom—apart when he rang up, or called, or emailed, or texted me, on any excuse, no matter how flimsy!

It was a way to keep 'tabs' on me...

I Was So Wrong!

Our second beautiful daughter, born four years after the first, had to be induced to be born, as I had gone three weeks over the projected date.

I believe that, subconsciously, I knew that she was safe where she was, so instinctively, I was protecting her for as long as possible from this harsh, strange world.

She had to be induced to be born, so I went into Burnley maternity hospital at 8 A.M., and, after the preliminaries, they began the injections, each of which brought on a labour pain. This continued until she was thankfully and warmly welcomed into the world at 1:10 A.M. the early hours of the following day.

Mr Graham, the obstetrician, then rang my home to inform my husband that she was safely delivered, but my husband didn't even answer the phone. We only had one phone then, no upstairs extension, but, at 1:15 A.M. in a very still, quiet house, it must have sounded very loud, and he must not have been sufficiently concerned to bother listening for it.

He said later that he didn't hear it!

But that was little consolation to me, having just come through childbirth, wondering where he was, and what he was doing!

My husband had hit our first daughter hard, even when she was 14 months old, standing in her cot crying to be lifted up and cuddled—I went into the room and witnessed this barbarism, staring like a rabbit paralysed in the headlights— and was more scared than I have ever been in my life! As I instinctively shouted and went forward to stop him, he turned and roughly pushed me away.

His excuse was that she was too much like his mother, and needed to be 'sorted out' as young as possible…

But, like a fool, I still thought that he would change for the better, eventually, and kept up the sham of a good marriage because my mother's friends all told me that the marriage wouldn't last, but I was determined to prove that it would…

My grandmother was right when she quoted, 'marry in haste, repent at leisure!'

I said that I would take charge of discipline, in order to protect them from his aggressive harshness—so, both our daughters thought that I was a disciplinarian and villain of the piece—they didn't know what he was capable of, and I didn't want them to find out the hard way.

This proved to be exceedingly difficult.

Whilst endeavouring to instil basic education and social skills in my daughters, I was hoping for the normality that I had searched for in my formative years. A sense of belonging, leading to security and independence, is what I aimed for, but we had to placate this man who would fly off the handle at the drop of a hat.

So we learned to try not to provoke him, which cut down on freedom of speech and action between us.

We also learned a kind of sign language that helped as a warning against his rising temper tantrums.

He tried desperately to make us conform to his rules, at the same time, he wanted all his own way.

He was an only child, and hadn't experienced sibling rivalry—I recognised this, and could see that his mother was fairly selfish, ruling the roost in her own home.

She told me that she hadn't enjoyed motherhood and possibly held her only child responsible for disrupting her lifestyle.

So, in my naivety, I thought that he would change, given good surroundings and treatment.

I was so wrong!

These people have an inborn disposition of control, and that's what they crave, no matter what the outcome…

My plan was for my daughters to grow up nicely, in a normal, courteous, well-mannered, intelligent family that had time to play together and have regard for each other's feelings. These were values that I wanted desperately as I grew up because my family was not the norm amongst my peers, and I felt that I could provide a security for my children that would in turn give them sufficient confidence to develop their own characters.

I was only young—18 years old when my first baby was born, and had never experienced punishment, so I was shocked to the core, didn't know how to deal with it. I even thought that this was how lots of people in the real world must have lived…because this was what my husband believed, and I knew that my childhood had been better than most of my peers.

I could always see that he hadn't known any different…and this is what I was determined to show him— that here was a happier way to live.

But he derived happiness in a malevolent, twisted, malicious way, that took me years to see.

My parents hardly had any discipline, my brother and I only received good treatment generally, so we didn't have the need/desire for rebellion. We had more freedom and slightly more luxury than the majority of our peers at school.

This severe, total control came very hard to me…

Maureen

One day, he asked me to make deeper pockets for his trousers because 'things kept falling out'.

It later transpired—through acquaintances—that his unisex barber had this rather well-endowed girl—twenty years his junior—that earned her money and gained popularity by pressing them into men's shoulders and breathing into their ears, as well as cutting hair.

Her husband, Jeff, touted for customers for her…such a nice family—not!

Maureen also had a back room for 'entertaining'. My husband used to say that as she only cut a minimal amount off, he had to go every other week!

This pleasure, he enjoyed in secret from me for ten years…this, under normal circumstances, I could have laughed off. However, these circumstances were not normal, as he used to fly into a rage if he thought he saw another man look at me, saying that it was my fault for being provocative.

This just was not true.

After enough of these occasions, and being told times without number that you don't look good, and are worthless, by a man who derives pleasure from drunken rages, you begin to believe it, and, instead of dressing up for fun, to go out and enjoy an evening with friends at the pub or restaurant, golf club, Masonic evenings, rugby club, etc., you think twice and begin to dress down.

I liked fun and dressing nicely—we sold fabric for a living and I used to make lots of my own clothes, and for my daughters when they were babies and toddlers. But I was young, and clung to the dream of wanting the ideal, secure marriage.

So, although I had lots of opportunities, chances and offers to go astray, I never did, partly because I was scared of the consequence if he discovered my straying, but mainly because I wouldn't spoil my daughters' image of their mother.

I felt that they were seeing too much bickering at home, and that was bad enough for them, without adding to their discomfort and sorrow.

So I lived in a world of my own as much as I could.

When I wasn't working, I kept myself busy by cooking and baking, sewing, knitting, playing the piano, painting and drawing, decorating, gardening and generally being a good housekeeper.

I say playing the piano…

I had piano lessons as a child, which I took up again when we bought a house that was big enough for a piano—and I became the owner a boudoir grand.

That was my pride and joy.

It was housed in a sort of garden lounge that we had, that had a huge 'picture window' that was the size of a shop front, from which could be seen lots of countryside, and it had a sprung, Canadian maple floor, which was brilliant for dancing. We had parties there, and when enough people were dancing in time to the beat of the music, you could feel the floor 'bounce' with rhythm!

There was a spacious view for miles across a valley in Yorkshire, and I loved to hear the music and allow it to float over the garden, fields and hedges.

However, as always, there was an ever-present fly in the ointment.

Roy used to say that one of his ambitions was to slam a piano lid down on the player's hands, so, I always stopped playing when he came near—although I knew it was another of his mind games.

I didn't wish to have my hands injured, and hear him explain to anybody else that the piano lid had accidentally fallen when I was playing!

And I knew that he was capable of doing it—just as part of his sick 'game'…

So, I played to my heart's content when I was in by myself, but never when he was in my vicinity…

He Never Actually Hit Me Whilst We Were Married

He never actually hit me whilst we were married. He always threatened to do, but he has gathered a fistful of my 'chest clothing' and drawn his other fist back in readiness.

I, at that point, said, "If you're going to hit me, make it a good one, because you'll never do it again…"

He let go, saying, "I won't give you the satisfaction of taking a bruise to the doctor or solicitor."

One Sunday afternoon, we had tickets to go to Caldervale Rugby Club charity event. So, we asked Roy's mother to sit in with the girls for us, so that we could go.

It was supposed to be a Tea Dance, but, knowing the rugby club lot, it turned into a Drinking Dance. This was before the drink/driving law came into existence.

So we all had a good time, and as I've always been able to enjoy dancing, and any kind of moving to music, I got lots of partners and it was a most entertaining and fun Sunday afternoon.

Roy had been stood drinking at the bar most of the time, and seemed to be enjoying himself. However, when we got into the car, and well on our way home, he suddenly started accusing me of dancing too much, and encouraging men to dance with me.

I knew to hold my tongue by this time, so didn't rise to the bait, but when we got back to our house, my inner feelings got the better of me, and I told his mother that he bullied me, and I found him to be scary.

She told me that I was being childish, and got into the car for him to take her home.

When he arrived back home, he had wound himself up into a temper and began ranting at me, chiefly on the lines of 'How dare you involve my mother in our private lives?' etc.

The girls, as usual, were there listening, which he knew upset me, as I didn't want them to witness all his hatred spewing out. But I stuck up for myself, and argued right back at him.

I happened to be standing below a step down into the kitchen, which was just covered in a kind of lino, quite a hard surface. He suddenly placed his hands on each of my shoulders, and pushed /threw me down onto this step, as violently as he could, using all of his very strong muscles and body and might. This hurt my back and tailbone in particular, and made me cry out with pain.

Once more, his actions had destroyed any vestige of trust and respect that I once had for him. Suddenly, he changed and seemed to realise what he had done, and was immediately profoundly sorry. But, by then, the physical and emotional damage had been done, and all the sorry in the world would never mend it.

He got enormous pleasure from making me cry. He has since admitted that he used to think of ways to make me cry as he drove home!

I could see how much pleasure he got from upsetting me, so I eventually had to harden myself against crying in front of him. He stopped me from crying at my brother's funeral, saying that I was showing him up.

He used to wear a gloating expression—a look of job satisfaction…when I was convulsed in tears, so I became slightly robotic, and learned to only ever cry when I was alone. He could always start an argument and turn it on to me, making me believe that it was my fault. The girls used to hear this, and side with him because he could always appear to be in the right.

I used to beg him not to start arguing in front of our daughters, but he would do it, just to prove that he could—it gave him a sense of 'ruling the roost' but taken to extremes.

This is how he tried to turn the girls against me.

And lying his way out of any situation was like a game to him—it was second nature which he found to be much more entertaining than telling the truth.

He would do anything to make me feel bad about myself—he practically invented subliminal messaging, so much so, that I can now almost recognise it from the next building!

He'd then become apologetic, abjectly wanting sympathy. But with the passage of time, I recognised that his earnest apologies were only part of his manipulative powers, and yet, he was such a plausible liar, and would do anything to get back into my good books, so that once again I would feel sympathy for him!

Once again, he would have gained the attention that he craved.

I knew he was sick and abnormal, so I did my best to help him, thinking that he would change and believing him when he said that this was the last time he would do it.

This always proved to be confidence sapping and energy draining. But there was always another day, another excuse for him to start a fight, till he wore me down and I learned how not to provoke him, whilst desperately hanging on to my self-belief and dignity.

He only ever hit me properly when I finally took courage in both hands and filed for divorce.

That story is in the chapter headed 'After the Divorce'!

Marian Butler

A school friend of mine, Marian Butler, was exceptionally good at sports. Her two brothers were enormously active in the local football and cricket scene, and worshipped all kinds of sporting events.

She was super fit, very much like them, taking pride in being long-legged, strong and supple and always featured most strongly in school team events such as hockey, basketball, swimming, running cross country, etc.

I lost touch with her, but still heard of her winning matches and trophies in spite of the fact that she was now married, with young children.

Her husband was a man of dubious character who had a reputation locally amongst northerners, as a 'wrong'un.' Chauvinism was quite common in the area, a throwback to the days when girls belonged to their fathers, who then handed them over to the husband.

Not too much thought or consideration went into the girl's education because it was recognised that a woman's place was in the home, and the man's job to go out into the world to earn money to keep the family and home together.

But Marian was different, with her tomboy ways and independence of thought.

That's why everybody was shocked to learn that she had drowned in an unbelievably tragic accident. The story was that she and her husband had been out in a dinghy on the local yachting lake, as they often did for recreation, and the orange, rubber dinghy had overturned in the exceptionally high wind, throwing the pair of them overboard. Only the husband had been able to climb back on the craft, when once it was righted, poor Marian fell afoul of the raging water and didn't survive...

Leaving her scheming husband to pick up her life insurance money, on a policy that had been newly taken out. Local yachts people said that it would have been virtually impossible for the man to climb back into the dinghy unaided because the craft was too lightweight, and would have simply overturned again if a man had tried to pull himself up and over the side.

So the locals said it was murder, but no one could ever prove it.

When my husband heard this, his eyes opened wide as he looked at me, and he said, "What a bloody, brilliant plan, how well-devised!"

This conveyed the message to me that he would like to emulate it. So from that day, I cancelled my life insurance policy because I wouldn't have him benefiting from my death in such a way, and I knew only too well that he was more than capable of it.

It would be fun for him to work out a similar plan, and he was obsessive enough to concentrate on getting it right—the main aim being to be without a witness, of course...

I have never had life insurance from that day onwards...

Electricity and Water

My ex-husband began his working life as an electrician, and whilst he was good at his job, he gradually developed the notion of idly wondering just exactly what would happen if a 'plugged in', live, electric fire were to drop in occupied bath water…

He never used this as a threat to me, but, the fact that he was mulling the idea over was sufficiently menacing to me.

The knowledge that this piece of foul play was in his head was enough to make me always ensure that the bathroom door was very firmly locked, whenever I indulged and luxuriated in deep, warm water. Using these 'mind games' was how he liked to keep me under some sort of control, and it was another source of sadistic pleasure to him. Again, if he had thrown a live hair-dryer, plugged in fan or electric fire into my bath water, he would have feigned innocence and explained to the police or anyone interested, as my own fault for dropping the appliance.

Thus, I knew full well that he would have got away with it because of his solidly determined, ability to act his way out of any given situation, display naivety, and put the blame onto anyone else but never himself.

Our detached house stood alone in farmland—our neighbours were some distance away. We had a cattle grid at the bottom of our drive, which our standard poodle (called Treacle because he was dark brown and sweet) could do a beautifully elegant, running, stretching leap over.

He extended all his four legs, flattened his ears to his head, appeared to grin with pleasure, and jumped far further than he needed to do!

Because he could, and because he liked to show off! He was a good, companionable dog, and I always felt secure in the isolated house when he was there.

I used to attend Rimington Women's Institute, to see some strong-minded, character-formed Yorkshire farmer's wives, who were the salt of the earth!

Watching Calendar Girls years later, always causes a lump in my throat, when I'm reminded of those times in that Skipton area.

We used to attend the local dinner dances at Stirk House, Gisburn, which was just a few miles away from where we lived, so we knew lots of locals, which made them good, social occasions.

This one in particular was most enjoyable, celebrating some local occasion.

We were amongst friends, the wine flowed, the small select band had played proper dance music, Roy propped the bar up, as usual, and I danced as much as I could—by myself if no one asked me, because I always loved it!

All was well, until we got home, and then he started.

"Why did you have to dance so much?"

"Because I can, and you don't want to do anything but stand at the bar drinking," I retorted.

He then began to issue threats that followed the line of, "I'll break both your f–ing legs, then you won't be able to do it again!" Not in a quiet voice, but bellowing as loudly as he could in my ear, whilst stamping about with a wild-eyed expression on his face.

This scared me so much, that I ran and grabbed the phone to call for help, but when I pressed the handset feverishly to my ear, it was stultifying soundless—just nothing there. No dialling tone or life of any sort, not even an echo of my voice.

It was then that I realised why he hadn't tried to stop me…

With astounding, heart stopping, stomach sinking amazement, I discovered that he'd unplugged the main phone downstairs—this upstairs one was just an extension and totally useless by itself!

All this time, he was shouting threats and bellowing insults at me, red faced and drunkenly wild eyed.

I knew from years of practical experience, that I had to get out of his way, allow his temper to run its course and subside. I also knew that by the following day, he would waken, remember his behaviour and be abjectly sorry.

A shallow, thoughtless man, to be pitied, on the face of it, but I was well aware that he just wanted the incident to be forgotten and glossed over, whilst he wallowed in self-pity and began to claim attention once more.

I managed to lock myself in the bathroom, and shouted back, "There won't be a next time because this finishes it. I'm going to leave you!"

This wasn't the first occasion that I'd had to barricade myself in for my own protection, nor the first house! I had always ensured that the bathrooms in all our houses had a good strong lock…

On this particular occasion, when I had been in the bathroom for some time, he quietened, sat on the floor near the door and began to apologise profusely and demonstrate true remorse—to the point where I could tell that his temper had abated and it was safe for me to emerge.

The following day, I said, "I am going to leave you if you won't have the decency to get out and leave me alone. I don't ever want to see you again, I don't like anything about you, you are abhorrent to me, and I can't stand you anymore!"

His reply was simple and to the point.

"I'd like to see you leave, taking all your dad's silver coins, Doulton and Moorcroft collection, etc., with you. You'll have to take it over my dead body because I'll stop you taking your possessions. If by any chance you do manage to go, I'll immediately change the locks, sell all your belongings and you'll never be able to see them again, let alone prove that they were ever yours!"

This was the norm in those days, and I had heard of this happening to women that walked out of their homes. Men were still very much regarded as the head of the household, and the law backed them up to that effect. I knew that he would love to do that, and it was possible because it's only comparatively recently that women have gained the same rights as men.

He also used to threaten to drive the car, with us both in it, at full speed into a brick wall, to kill the pair of us, rather than allow me to win.

I wasn't going to allow to him get away with all his abominable behaviour, my possessions, and leave me stranded, after all I'd done for him.

I decided I'd bite the bullet for a little longer, continue to enjoy my lifestyle despite him, and bide my time…

The Dolly Tub and the Silver

My mother had inherited a dolly tub.

This was a very big, round, aluminium receptacle, of hip-height, that was used for doing the family washing, long before washing machines were invented.

Monday was usually set aside for washing day—such a long, arduous process, that began by heating sufficient water in the boiler, then ladling it from there, with a lading can, into the tub to fill it at least three-quarters full.

Next, the soap powder was added and dissolved by stirring. The clothes would be sorted into whites, coloureds and darks, and washed in that order, so that the darkest clothes used the dirtiest water—it didn't matter because it wouldn't show!

All the ritual pounding, rinsing, and wringing would clean them anyway…

Clothes went through the mangle—turned by hand—between each wash and rinse, which was exceedingly labour intensive!

The clothes were turned and agitated in the water by means of a dolly—a long wooden handle attached very firmly to what looks like a small three-legged stool.

Some lucky person had the job of turning it and swirling the water through the various clothes, to encourage the unwanted particles of dirt to leave the fabric and enter the water!

This water then had to be tipped out, or emptied by hand and ladling can!

Then there was the starching, drying and ironing to be done, but I'll leave those processes to your imagination—no electric irons or fancy stuff like that remember!

But suffice it to say that pride was gained by having the whitest whites and the stiffest collars!

All in all, a very hot, steamy, difficult, heavy procedure, calling for the utmost stamina, determination and strong muscles!

This old dolly tub, stood, largely unnoticed, in a corner of our, quite big, garage, for years. It had some old carpet thrown casually over it, and it was just forgotten.

However, one day, my dad was having a new boiler installed—changing from the existing coke one, to a modern gas fired boiler.

The workmen came to him and said that they'd have to move the dolly tub, to get at the pipes.

"That's OK," said my dad, "you don't need my permission—just do it!"

"We would," said our local friendly plumbers, "we've tried, but it's just too heavy to move—we can't budge it!"

My dad couldn't understand why these two, young, burly men couldn't move it, so went to investigate.

He lifted out all the bits of old carpet and discovered, to his total amazement, that it was over half full of old silver coins, that he had no knowledge of whatsoever!

When he told my mother, she just laughed and said that she'd been waiting to see how long it would take for her hoard to be discovered!

Then, she explained, that long ago, she had heard that silver coins were replaced by nickel in 1945.

Up to then, they'd been approximately half silver from 1921, and before then, they were composed of almost all silver. So she'd decided to collect them from our 'takings'. She used to always go through the money that we drew from selling textiles, take out any from below these dates and drop them into the old dolly tub.

She'd put a piece of carpet in there initially, to deaden the sound!

Her cousin and her husband, Olive and Dick Gorton, had a butcher's shop in the perimeter of Accrington market hall and they used to indulge her by saving her these coins, for which she repaid them in 'modern' currency.

She also knew other shopkeepers, and persuaded them to keep their old silver for her, in exchange for the up to date coinage that she gave them.

They humoured her and treated it as a joke, so she was able to accumulate the silver fairly quickly, thus building quite a collection, as a harmless, purposeful, hobby.

When she died, my father still didn't touch the collection. He thought it was highly amusing that she'd been able to do this unseen and unheard!

He also realised that no burglar could steal it because it was just too big and heavy!

So there it stood for another ten years or so, until he'd had the first of his strokes, which made him realise that he needed to set his affairs in order.

So he asked me to take over the coin collection.

We had a large garage at our house in Middop, near Gisburn, so, little by little—I did!

They took a long time to be moved—carrier bag by carrier bag!

Whilst we were doing this, my husband befriended a coin dealer, who was willing to exchange them, in smallish amounts, for folding-type money, which we used towards carpeting and furnishing our house.

It also helped towards financially supporting Roy for the best part of twenty years, in which he refused to seek employment, when once my dad died.

I was the sole beneficiary.

How I wish I had my dolly tub full of silver back now!

John and Carol's Wedding

I have written some accounts of my experiences of being married to a psychopath, but there are many, many more!

One that I now recall, at first seems funny, but shows the extent that these fiends will go to for their own amusement.

We had been to the wedding of my cousin John and Carol—Carol turned out to be a very good friend.

This celebration took place in Sawston Hall, in the village of Sawston, near Cambridge

Our two little daughters, Dianne and Carolyn, were bridesmaids, and a friend of Carols had made their salmon-pink, satin dresses.

The satin was heavy and the fitted, long dresses were plain at the front but had an insert of frills down the back of the skirt—because they would be seen chiefly from the back as they walked down the aisle and stood at the altar.

Lots of preparation had gone into the wedding and I had bought the best, most expensive outfit I had ever had.

We arranged to stay at the Rutland Arms in Newmarket, for a couple of nights, and my dad was there with my Aunt Carrie and Uncle Billy. The atmosphere was of a huge party right from the word go, because Carols parents, Peggy and Fred Bright were extremely generous, and nothing was too much trouble for them. Carol was their only child, and they wanted her to have the best that they could provide.

The day dawned, with a clear blue sky and sunshine.

The bride was beautiful and radiant, the groom was proud and at peace with the world, and our daughters looked like moving pictures from a story book, acting out a much-loved fairy tale.

The wedding went well, the Church was full of flowers, people, music, light and happiness.

After the ceremony, we were able to walk from the church, to the reception, which was held in Sawston Hall. A brilliant occasion, in which nothing was spared to make it go as well as was possible, that everyone enjoyed to the utmost.

It's fresh in my mind yet, as a jewel of a day, in which we were all treated like royalty, and felt privileged to attend.

However, once again, there is a secret, which I have in my heart, that the guests would have found fascinatingly horrific, yet hilarious, if only I'd let them in on it.

But, once again, I kept quiet because I didn't want them to know that our marriage was anything but 'normal', whatever that is!

Until now, when I feel ready to disclose yet another example of the extent of the sadism, that he gained pleasure from.

The Brown Suede Trilby

Fred and Peggy Bright, Carol's parents, were the most generous people I had ever met—apart from my dad, and extremely hospitable to say the least. Nothing was ever too much trouble for them, we only had to admire something, and they wanted to give it to us.

So we had to choose our words very carefully.

Our daughters, Dianne and Carolyn, were staying with them for two or three days, so that their dresses could be given a final fitting by the dressmaker.

I'd never left them for more than a few hours at a time with anyone else, so it was quite a wrench for me to leave them, as part of my heart stayed with them.

I knew that they would be looked after very well, cosseted and spoilt, but I still didn't like being parted from them, because I enjoyed their company.

So, I must have delayed leaving them as long as possible, even to the point of ignoring my call of nature to the bathroom. We duly said our goodbyes, hugged our last hugs and kissed our last kisses, left them and headed for home. When we'd been traveling for an hour or more, I asked if we could stop at a café or store, so that I could 'Spend a penny'.

"We'll stop when the traffic and conditions allow," said Roy, "surely, you can wait!"

I knew how easily provoked he was, so I waited, not wanting an argument whilst I was concentrating on controlling my bladder!

Another hour went by, and I know he usually liked to drive until he arrived at his destination, but, as this was a four-hour journey, I felt sure that he'd like a break.

The driving continued, and my need for bladder relief grew greater…

When we approached our usual stopping place for tea, toast and comfort, I said, "Please stop here, I'm desperate for the loo!"

"I don't want to stop here," he said, "we'll stop later."

But of course, he kept relentlessly driving the car telling me that he had made arrangements to play golf at a pre-arranged time, and because I'd taken too long to say my 'farewells', it had put him on the deadline for the timing of his game.

This upset me, as it was the first I'd heard about it. He'd found yet another way to make me suffer, that could look as though I'd had an 'accident'.

A casual observer would never believe that he had refused to find time for me to stop and visit the 'ladies' to 'spend a penny'.

He would make them believe that my water-works were uncontrolled because he was such a good actor.

By now, I was becoming distressed and had to take urgent action.

I was perilously near to wetting myself and terrified of it happening.

I looked around the interior of our dark brown Singer Vogue estate car for inspiration, when my eyes fell upon Roy's brand-new, dark brown, suede, trilby hat that he was very fond of and enjoyed wearing.

Yes, you've guessed it!

We were driving on a country road, hardly any traffic about, and the next built up area was miles away—typical Yorkshire countryside.

I climbed into the back, much to my husband's unbelieving, torrential stream of words, as he realised what I was about to do. I placed the upturned hat in the well of the car, straddled it, braced myself, and gratefully relieved my poor, stretched bladder into the trilby!

Oh, the blissful relief that I felt was worth vastly much more than a penny!

(But it's not easy in a moving vehicle with restricted room between the seats—you should try it sometime!)

It was a very good quality hat, one of Ahernes of Hellifields finest, that I had bought for his birthday present, and it held the hot liquid well!

Ten out of ten for good workmanship and materials!

The car was still in motion, so I daren't leave the 'receptacle' on the floor or it would sway and splash over...

As soon as the thought entered my brain, I knew the only solution!

The windows were the wind-down variety (Yes, you're correct again!), so I wound down the nearside one.

Next, the hat and contents, which came almost to the brim, were slowly, carefully and gingerly lifted. I had to balance the unusual suede container, so as not to allow its' cargo of swirling liquid to sluice over the sides of the vessel.

I placed the lot at arm's length out into the rapidly moving, windy, air stream and dropped it!

Sorry, Yorkshire, but he didn't give me an option!

I often wondered what further indignities that hat suffered. It may have been picked up by a farmer's boy, who wondered why it smelt funny, washed it, then wore it, until it ended up atop a scarecrow!

Whatever its' fate, it did me a great service that day—it was worth every penny that I paid for it, and I'm eternally grateful to it...

Three cheers for good, brown, suede trilbies!

Castercliffe

My dad realised that all the men in his family had either died when they were aged seventy, or before.

This spurred him to plan for his retirement, by having a bungalow built by a local farmer he had befriended.

It was on Tum hillside overlooking a valley. This was an area that the Romans visited, excavated and quarried and they named it Castercliffe.

So the bungalow was named after it, built into the hillside and only accessible for the last 200 yards or so by a track.

He had walked round there almost every day—or whenever possible—all the time he lived in Colne.

My father began having series of minor strokes when he reached the age of seventy, and the doctor explained that each one destroyed a small part of his brain.

His strokes came more frequently as time went by, so that at one point he came out of hospital and had to be assessed as to whether he was fit to live alone and capable of living a normal life without injuring himself accidentally.

He wasn't well at all, very tired most of the time and sleeping a lot.

He had difficulty walking and his memory was fast receding.

But he still had three years to go before he eventually died of pneumonia.

I visited him two or three times a day, taking meals for him, cleaning, doing his shopping and laundry, before it got too much for me and he came to live with us to give me more time.

One day, whilst he was still living in his bungalow, we called to take care of him, to do whatever was necessary to help him, and he had put a pillow on the kitchen table, rested his head on it, and was fast asleep.

My husband looked long, hard and thoughtfully at him, and said meaningfully, "It wouldn't take much to put him out of it now, press his head down hard into the pillow—it won't take long."

"I'm going out for a walk now, I'll be back in half an hour, and I expect you to have done it by the time I return…"

I was horror-struck, mortified and very distressed at this cold, deliberate, heartless instruction, and as I stared disbelievingly, he neared the door, stopped, turned around to look at us, and said, "Good-bye, Harry!"

I sat close to my dad, watching and listening to his steady, relaxed, clear, childlike breathing as he slept, I remembered all he had taught me about life, and how good and generous he had always been to me, and never even hinted at being annoyed with anything I did.

I received lots of encouragement and gained much confidence from him.

He had stood by me and allowed me to have all the freedom it was possible to have in our limited existence, and always made work as much fun as possible.

He would turn up with little gifts, never expecting anything in return but friendship, so I could never, ever do anything to hurt him, in any way at all.

Quite the reverse.

My instinct was to protect him at all times, particularly at times like this when he was weak, fragile, vulnerable and totally unable to defend himself.

I heard Roy's footsteps as he returned from his walk when the half an hour had passed, making fear rise into my throat and my heart began to pound in my eardrums and chest so loudly that the sound seemed to fill the room.

With trepidation, I held my breath with a jittery, fearful, heart-stopping anxiety.

I had no idea what mood he would be in when he discovered that I hadn't carried out his instruction, and that my dad was still peacefully asleep—and alive.

He opened the door and entered the room.

Staring in amazement and disbelief at us, he said, "You didn't manage to do it then? Why not? This was a perfect opportunity!"

No answer sprang to my lips this time. I couldn't bear to have yet another heated quarrel over such an incredibly awful, dreadfully sensitive, subject just now, as I knew only too well how volatile Roy's temper was, and how determined he would be to tell me that he was right, no matter what the circumstances were.

So I kept quiet, ignored Roy's words and stayed that way until my dad wakened naturally.

If I had killed my father, as Roy wanted me to do, he would have absolved himself from all responsibility. He would have laid the blame squarely on me because, with his very well-practiced straight face, he would have denied all knowledge of the horrific, terrible incident to anyone else.

And no one would ever guess that he had been the instigator of the murder.

How he imagined that I could ever suffocate my dad, who'd never even spoken a wrong word to me in my life, let alone treat me anything but good and kindly, I'll never know, and have wondered about since that day.

My dad had given us both the same generosity that he had always done, and Roy admitted that he was much happier with my father than he was with his own.

He said that the act would have, "Put your dad out of his misery," but how he thought that I could have lived with that awful memory, along with all the others that he had given me, was beyond my reasoning.

So ruthlessly rigid and callous, with such an utterly, total lack of concern for others, is again one of the traits of a psychopath.

As my brother had been killed in a car accident, I was the only beneficiary from my fathers will, so he would get access to any money quicker that way, rather than waiting for events to happen naturally.

My dad went into a retirement home shortly afterwards, because I had coped with him at our house with extreme difficulty, for as long as I could.

But the strain of all this became too much for me, he had become doubly incontinent, along with the business, family and the control put upon me by my husband.

He was in the retirement home for some time, which gave me much relief as he gradually deteriorated.

Then, one day, he was left standing by himself and fell onto the side of a cabinet, breaking two ribs.

Eventually, he died in the hospital.

In time, we sold off the bungalow, and house, which sound quite grand for my standards, but this was in Lancashire, 1983, when house prices were still low countrywide, and even lower in Lancashire!

I was the sole beneficiary, and had been since my brother's death, so there came a day when my dad's assets were realised and the money was in our joint bank account.

At this point, my husband went around the house, lifting his face and arms up to heaven and then allowing his arms and hands to fall down, slapping noisily on his thighs, saying very loudly,

"It's not enough! It's not enough!"

Over and over again…till, once more, I felt sick at his reaction.

Within a year or so, my husband sold off the business. By this time, textiles were going out of fashion as masses of cheap, good clothing was coming in from the third world.

The government paid local mills to close and sold the machinery, looms and orders to the third world, where, incidentally they didn't reckon with the weather differences.

The weather in Lancashire is very wet and damp, so the cotton thread was pliable and would stretch a little.

In India, Pakistan, etc., the climate is very dry and hot, so when cotton spinning and weaving was attempted, the thread-

lacked moisture, became brittle, and snapped easily, thus halting production time considerably.

However, back to my story. At this point, instead of looking round for other means of employment, he announced that he was going to retire, which he did.

He played lots of golf, holing in one six times, which demonstrates the amount of dedication he applied to the game, and the amount of games he had to play to reach that status!

Two men, who were neighbours of ours, Roger and David, in succession, offered him three mornings cleaning their works, and he felt that he couldn't refuse because then they would openly ridicule him.

The work was forced upon him, and he didn't like the situation, but couldn't get out of it without losing face. He was sacked by each of them, and didn't work again until we moved south where I took courage in both hands and filed for divorce. But, he virtually had almost twenty years of retirement, from when my father died, and he has never once thanked me for those years of idleness…

The Everlasting Arguments

The everlasting arguments begin to wear you down, to the point where you become robotic, giving standard answers, so as not to provoke an argument, and you stop believing in yourself.

This happens to women in all walks of life!

Maybe men too, but I don't know any.

Whilst I've been writing this book, and decided to be open about it, lots of women have confided in me, and we share a varied number of events, varying depths and methods of abuse, but mainly, we share the same fears and destruction of confidence

These psychopaths are very clever, and well-skilled in their craft of control.

Mine never gave me a witness, ever…

He would glare at me from across a crowded room, if he thought that no-one was looking, but he always saved his black side for when we were behind locked doors.

Too much of a coward to show his true colours in public.

Too much of a bully to stop his overwhelming urge to control.

He was always charming, helpful and entertaining when other people were present, thus no one suspected how dark his other side was.

He's a very accomplished actor—

- as was his domineering mother, who was recorded in her advancing years by Burnley hospital as being a very plausible liar!

She subjugated his father, who was never allowed to speak freely whilst she was there, so he'd almost lost the ability to speak at all.

As soon as he plucked up courage, removed his pipe from his mouth and spoke the first three words of a sentence, she would interrupt, and finish his statement as she saw fit, regardless of whether it was what he wanted to say, telling him he was wrong, and causing whoever was present, to laugh at him.

He was a gentle character, who always gave in to her for the sake of a quiet life—and besides, she was bigger than him!

When we moved to a house that had an acre of garden, he used to enjoy coming up to the house to help with the gardening, and, it was there, for the first time, that he and I had been alone together.

I kept fairly quiet, and he talked, about all sorts of things.

Often about his childhood, telling me that his mother had been in service at a big house, and that she was a good cook.

He also said that he'd always wanted to have a go at baking, but had never had the chance.

I told him that he could use all my stuff, and cook or bake at our house, but he always declined, saying he was too old and it was too late.

So he went through his married life, denying himself any pleasures, because she wouldn't like it!

Floristry

I'd always loved gardens and plants, so I decided to train as a florist.

I got City & Guilds in Floristry, City & Guilds in Flower Arranging and the City & Guilds 730 Adult Teaching Certificate.

I joined the local National Association of Flower Arranging Societies, and found the local Forest of Pendle Flower Club committee—becoming the chairman of it for three years, and trained to become a demonstrator to Flower Clubs.

This meant that I had to find my way round the North West Area to reach these clubs, so it got me out of the house, gave me confidence and I began to feel the scent of independence again after a lifetime (or so it seemed!) of subjugation.

I gained more qualifications and made lots of new friends, which was just what I needed.

I worked for florists for some time, eventually buying my own shop.

The premises were just the right size, not too big or small, with an upstairs and a cellar, which was always cold, because a stream ran through it.

Roy put a new shop counter in for me, but because I'd said that any money I made from the shop was to be mine—he wouldn't do anything else, as he wasn't going to get money from it!

I worked very hard to make it look good—painting, cleaning, polishing, etc.—whilst giving the customers the best service that I could.

When I thought the time was right, I applied for an Interflora agency.

I knew that it was a forlorn hope as I'd only had the shop for a year and it wasn't up to standard, but I also knew that the inspection would clarify where I needed to work and improve.

It also needed to be better established.

The day came that the Interflora man came round, chatted nicely and pointed out the main points that were needed to gain the agency, letting me know very gently that I wasn't ready yet.

This didn't come as a surprise to me, as I'd been working in an Interflora shop and knew just how high the standards had to be.

Roy had kept saying that I would get it and wouldn't listen to any other way of thinking.

When I went home and told him that I hadn't got it yet, his words were, "Shall I kick your bollocks off now or wait a while?"

Let me hasten to assure you that I don't have those appendages! But, because he was so chauvinistic, this was how he thought and spoke!

He'd always refused to help in the shop, other than dire necessities e.g. deliveries on Mother's Day.

This made me realise how much I hated him. That's when I filed for divorce for the first time.

I filed for divorce for the first time in 1995, and got my decree nisi.

My plan was to go down south, near my exceedingly hard-working daughter, where I could help her with her young daughter, and leave him up north to continue to play golf and go out with his pals.

He used to express distaste whenever I suggested moving south, so I thought this arrangement would suit us both.

However, when I told my daughter of my intentions, she said, "We'd love you to come down here, but don't come by yourself, 'cos we don't have time to put shelves up for you and help you in any way!"

So, what with that little bombshell, and him walking round the place shouting about, "How could you?" I relented and again bit the bullet to stay with him.

We did move south, and stood at some Antique Fairs, mainly selling off what was left of my dad's collections.

Our daughter presented us with a baby grandson, a brother for our granddaughter, in each of whom we were delighted.

The divorce had shown him that I really was very hurt and needed more freedom, so he became more tolerable. However, leopards can't change their spots, and he did have many, many lapses.

One day, we were looking after our grandson who was two years old, and his sister was at school.

He had a rotten cold, and, as the weather was cool, he was wearing a heavy sweater.

My husband had just heard of 'bonding' and decided that this would be the day that he bonded seriously with the little boy.

He had the child sat on his knee for most of the day, except when they had a game on the floor, and I could see that the baby was far too hot.

I suggested removing his heavy sweater, and moved towards them to do it, but Roy pushed me away, saying, "Go away, we don't want you!" And making the baby laugh, by his 'game'.

In a little while, I could see that our two-year-old grandson was red-faced and sweating uncomfortably, so I wetted a sponge with cold water, and wanted to wipe his face, but was yet again met with the same response, "Go away, we don't want you!" which was a typical game he played for his own amusement.

By this time, I couldn't bear to watch him 'bonding' any longer, so I took my watercolour equipment into the dining room, and sat immersed in my painting, where I couldn't see them.

The next thing I knew was when my husband frantically brought the lifeless body of our grandson in to me, and said, "Look at him—what can I do?"

At this, I was absolutely horrified, I couldn't believe what had happened, and quickly rang 999.

A young man who was very capable, and well-trained, answered the call quickly.

He had to calm me down first and get a lucid story out of me, because I was panicking at this time, but he did get the facts from me, assured me that an ambulance was on its way, and meanwhile, he instructed me to do what I'd wanted to do two hours earlier—that is remove the child's clothing, including his nappy and sponge him with cold water.

The ambulance arrived within minutes, diagnosed a fit—brought on by excessive heat, and the very capable staff took him to hospital—accompanied by my husband, who was distraught by this time, realising what he'd done.

I was trembling now, and had to face telling my daughter and her husband, but, as usual, I said it must have been accident. Thus, shielding my husband from the truth, and not wanting to upset my daughter and her husband any more that they were already upset by the child's illness.

He, as always, wouldn't admit the truth because he couldn't stand to be seen in a bad light, and stuck to the story of it being an accident, but, in truth, it was done purely for his own benefit.

To satisfy his ego, show me that he was in charge, and to bond with his grandson,

He just hadn't reckoned on the exceedingly dangerous outcome.

Working Together

When my brother, Derek, died in a car crash, my world was shattered because I'd always looked up to him for help and guidance.

He was six years older than me, and often had to be my chaperone when my parents were busy.

I missed him dreadfully when he was taken from me so suddenly, and without warning.

My husband was not upset by this incident, even to the point of telling me to stop crying at Derek's funeral, saying, "You're showing me up!"

He thought that I would have to rely on him more—therefore, increasing his hold on me.

He told me that he'd like to join the family business, and asked me to persuade my father to allow him in—-which my dad did—-albeit reluctantly, as he couldn't very well refuse under the circumstances, and I think he knew that I was being bossed around unnecessarily

Working and living together increased the level at which I had to be vigilant.

I didn't get much time to myself ever, and tried to escape into my world of 'Being a Good Mother', by looking after the children, sewing, knitting, cooking, drawing, gardening and decorating etc.

He always did any work that my dad wanted him to do, filling and emptying vans of cloth, checking lists of the fabrics, and helping with the wholesale customers, sorting out the warehouses etc.

We also stood markets, which were good fun when I was young, but became a drag after doing it for years. On Saturdays, we would unpack and set up three stalls with fabrics of all kinds, and then Roy would clear off to play golf for the day!

Leaving me with just a young Saturday girl for help. I didn't argue because it meant that he would be away from me for most of the day, so all the hard work was the price I had to pay to have my own thoughts and feelings.

Also, we used to go to the Golf Club on Saturday nights, when they held dinner dances.

I made the most of the dancing—which I loved—having quite a few partners.

Needless to say, he wasn't too keen on this, and I had to be very wary, not knowing what mood he'd be in when we went home at the end of the evening.

Following me round the house, bellowing in my ear, pushing me—often into the wall—were all part of the more usual ways that he vented his feelings and tantrums. I used to lock myself in the bathroom until he calmed down.

He once drove off from the local pub at Blacko that we were drinking in with the crowd of friends, leaving me on the Rising Sun car park at 1 o'clock in the morning.

I had asked for the car keys so that I could drive home as he had had far too much to drink.

Thus, I had to walk the two and a half miles' home to Middop, dressed in a skimpy summer dress, high heels and swinging my handbag on a country road, lit only by the stars and moonlight!

Again, it was something that I would never choose to do because it was a very frightening experience, but I was determined not to let it get the better of me! It was different, eerily enjoyable and utterly memorable!

I will never forget it!

Trees creaked, dry stone walls appeared to have faces, shadows were scary, the moonlight gave everything a translucent appearance, and oh, the relief when the occasional cars went safely by without stopping, leaving me alone and unscathed!

Luckily, I survived—remembering his words, "If ever you're raped, don't bother coming back home!"

When I finally reached our detached house in the country, where the nearest neighbour was some distance away, the house was in total darkness.

I let myself in, and he stubbornly pretended to be asleep and never apologised or gave a sign of remorse or showed that he had any feelings of sympathy towards me.

But, like so many of the others, I could never forget the incident.

My Big Toe!

The ball joint of my big toe had developed arthritis, because I was once carrying a bucket of water when the handle broke and the bucket dropped on to that joint.

It became painful, so I went to the hospital and the surgeon said that he could tidy the joint and make it more comfortable.

This I had done.

I came round in the little ward, still with a drip attached, a nurse in attendance and my foot bound up.

A couple of hours later, I had had a drink of tea and eaten a slice of toast, when my husband came bounding into the room saying, "Come on, I thought you'd be ready by now. You'll have to hurry up because I've parked badly and need to get out of the car park quickly."

At this, the little nurse began to panic, because this is the effect he has on people, and she said to me, "You'll have to spend a penny before you leave as that's a requirement. We have to show that you're eating and drinking normally, and that your bladder is working before you can leave—so here are your crutches—I'll help you into the bathroom!"

"Then I'll help you to get dressed."

This happened so quickly, and I had only just had my drip removed and must still have been full of the general anaesthetic, because when I swung my legs out of bed, I automatically put both feet on the ground to steady myself, feeling the newly operated on joint crack somehow.

I wasn't in a fit state to hold a conversation, let alone argue, so that's just another incident that I had to live with and keep quiet about so as not to incur his wrath

When I later pointed out to him that he didn't even bother to ask me how I was after the operation, he said, "I asked the nurse outside if you were fit to leave hospital and she said yes. So that's how I knew you could come out."

No apology—and the fact that he'd been callous, brusque and devoid of any feeling for anyone except himself, didn't even enter his mind.

The toe joint is just as bad now—or worse—than it was before…

My husband was quite helpful for most of the time, although I always had to watch his face to see what mood he was in, so that I knew not to provoke him, and he tried his best to be like other men, but for about a quarter of the time we were married, I had to be very wary of him and almost learnt to tread on egg shells without breaking them.

He had a ruthless lack of concern for others, totally without conscience, quite remorseless, obsessive and needed to be securely on a pedestal at all times.

All I wanted, was for him to leave me alone, when once the marriage was at the point of no return, but he could never do this.

I used to lie wide awake in the same bed as him, at my wits end, crying, and trying to work out why he got so much pleasure from hurting me, and what was the best thing to do.

All he did was to tell me to, "Shut up, you're keeping me awake!"

Too frightened to tell anyone that I'd married a lout, because I knew that they wouldn't believe me as he was so nice and affable when in company.

I was not willing to walk out leaving him in a luxury house that my family had paid for, and filled with quality goods because he said that if I did, he'd sell everything and keep the money for himself.

So, we had twin beds for the last twenty years of our marriage, and I had my own room for the last five.

100

A big part of his game was to torment and tease me, and make sure that no one else suspected.

He was/is, such a plausible liar, and such a good actor, that he brought this state of affairs about.

Entirely at my expense—both financially and emotionally.

Even after the divorce, which he never thought I'd have the courage carry through, he was so humiliated and upset at being left alone, that he went crying to all our family and friends, saying effectively, "How could she do such a thing to me? I've no idea why she's divorced me, I'm so deeply unhappy without her…"

Without ever giving a thought to the unhappiness that he'd deliberately caused me over a virtual lifetime, merely to satisfy his own feeling of sadistic pleasure.

Yet, never willing to leave me alone and find a life for himself.

The Divorce

I wondered every day why he was very often as awkward as he could be, and why he derived such pleasure from being this way.

It couldn't be deprivation because we never had any money worries whilst my dad was around, and third world children haven't any possessions at all, but that doesn't turn them into psychopaths.

It seems that these people are born with it, their genes don't work together properly so they don't experience the same emotions as us because there's something missing in their brain-like colour blindness.

He had no hesitation in creating a hostile environment for me wherever and whenever there wasn't a witness. It came just naturally to him, and I don't think he realised how deeply damaging to me it was, and the amount of effort I had to summon up to tolerate it.

Because I had tried so hard with him, and we shared all I had, he had come to rely on me more that I realised. When the time came for me to gather all my courage and go for a divorce, to say that I was frightened is a super understatement!

I wasn't aware then of the number of women that have been/are killed by men—chiefly their husbands—it was on average, two per week...

He used to tell me repeatedly that I wasn't fit to live by myself, I'd never cope and that if ever I dreamed of leaving him, he'd come after me and, "Break your legs before I break your f–king neck!"

So, I well remember making the divorce papers out in secret.

I had to wait until he'd gone out for a newspaper or something, then do a page or as much as I could before he returned, because he was so possessive and obsessive, that he wanted to know what I was doing at all times.

In time, I completed the papers and will never forget the moment that I let my small grandson post them, because that was when I anticipated that the fireworks would start.

The flock of butterflies in my tummy started a flying riot, and I got a huge heavy period that was very abnormal, as my periods had begun to lessen considerably, due to my age.

The doctor rushed me into hospital for a check-up, and, when I came round from the general anaesthetic, the surgeon said that there was nothing physically wrong, but that I had an excess of adrenalin (or whatever it is that triggers a period to begin), that he could only put down to over excitement or similar. And he agreed that fear came under the same heading. So I had physical proof that fear can have an adverse effect on flesh and blood.

He knew it was wrong, and used to threaten me with all sorts if I dared to tell anyone.

I wanted the ideal life—as we all do—and as he was largely OK, a good handyman, basically faithful apart from minor dalliances—(because he knew that if he went with another woman and I found out, that would end it), loyal and handled the money well, I found it easier to stay with him and do my own thing, living more like brother and sister than husband and wife, because I knew that the financial situation provided me with security, and I wasn't going to be silly enough to walk away leaving him in the comparative luxury that my family had provided, after I had taken all the abuse for years.

I wanted security for my old age…

I hadn't realised just how strongly and fiercely he had become dependent on me, making him very reluctant to allow me to leave him.

But I more and more began to know that I just couldn't go into old age with him because if ever I was ill, I didn't want my last view of the world to be one of him coming towards me with a pillow.

He had no regret or remorse about urging me to suffocate my dad when he was ill, just disappointment when I wouldn't do it, so I couldn't spend the rest of my life dreading the day that I became too weak to defend myself, and was alone with him…

I knew that the time had come to break out and get away, no matter what the cost…

When the divorce papers were delivered to him, and he finally realised that I was quite determined to go ahead, he became abjectly distraught, saying that he would kill himself, but for the fact that it would mean he would never be able to see me again!

I knew that this was just another ploy, but to humour him, and so that I didn't have his death on my conscience, I took him to our doctors, at Mount Chambers in Braintree.

She was very understanding, and as he sat there in her surgery, crying and weeping crocodile tears of remorse and regret into her box of tissues, she told me that I, or anyone else, couldn't be responsible for him killing himself.

Neither could we prevent him from suicide if this was what he was going to do.

I was, and still am, extremely grateful to her, for level headed, good, support, common sense and understanding.

Tolerating a Psychopath

Tolerating a psychopath is like feeding an illness—they're determined to win at all cost, and by showing them tolerance and understanding, they think that they've achieved their goals easily.

Satisfied that they are the eternal victors, they become frustrated when they meet resilience next time, under the same circumstances, regardless of right or wrong, because their main aim is to be top dog, no matter what.

A good friend of mine, Beryl, likens users to a dog under the table, waiting for crumbs. They're OK as long as you don't run out of food.

They have an unshakeable ego as big as a house, and imagine that their way is the right way in all things.

In précis;

You should never fight with a pig,

Because it hurts, you get covered in the pig's dirt, and the pig enjoys it!

He'd always tried to rule by intimidation and subjugation, telling me that I wasn't capable of living alone and that if I ever left home, he'd come after me and break my legs then my neck!

My parents bought a little four-roomed cottage for us, and paid to have it modernised.

They replaced the drains in the backyard and a new toilet, gave us furniture and decoration, including a new fireplace.

I'll never forget my husband standing with his back to the window, and stating, "You know that police won't come out to a call for domestic violence, don't you?"

I was eighteen years old, pregnant, never heard of domestic violence, and hadn't a clue what he was talking about.

But I was about to find out...

Also early on in the marriage, he told me that if ever I was raped,

"Don't bother to come home!"

This was when I was young, trying my best in every way, and had two daughters to care for and protect from him...

Breaking up then, would have meant that my dad's small family business would be in jeopardy,

As my brother had been killed in a car crash, Roy replaced him, and we needed all the hands we could get to make it run.

My husband knew this, felt that he was indispensable, and used it as a whip hand.

He knew that I wanted to be loyal to my dad and daughters, so he saw it as a way to blackmail me to get his own way

A few years ago, a man called Frederick West was brought to trial, convicted and sent to prison for life. He was found guilty of killing several young girls and burying them in concrete in his cellar, with his wife, Rosemary's, help.

My husband said that Frederick West would be praised and feted in jail, and the inmates would hold him up and regard him as a hero...

Now I'm not familiar with the 'goings on' in jail, but I can't see this being the case.

It certainly went beyond my imagination, but who knows how these twisted minds work.

Many, many years later, I allowed my four-year-old grandson, to post my divorce papers—lifting him up to the letter box—because the flashpoint that determined me to get out of the marriage for good, was when Roy shouted, threatened and reduced the child to sobbing tears for eating a chocolate biscuit on the settee, instead of sitting up to the table and using a plate!

After the Divorce

After the divorce, he still couldn't leave me alone. Because his house wasn't ready, he had to move in with me in the little house that I had chosen to be my safe haven.

Throughout the marriage, I had to be under constant scrutiny, having to explain my every action.

This I tolerated, putting it down to his upbringing.

His mother was obsessive and his father almost couldn't breathe without having to explain why.

After two months of him still under my roof—-even though he was helping with the decorating etc., I got fed up of this 'more of the same' feeling.

He blamed his solicitors, so, one day I rang them to find out what the delay was.

I was shocked and horrified when they told me that my ex-husband had told them to 'drag it out as long as possible!'

So I told them the truth, they completed everything within a week, and he finally and mercifully, moved out into his own house.

He didn't have a mortgage on his pretty house; he had tens of thousands in the bank, working, and was sitting pretty.

But he wasn't happy with his own company.

Never has been, and never will be.

Also, after the divorce, he was surprised to find himself alone! He never thought that I would have the courage to go through with it, so he didn't envisage the consequences.

Suddenly, he was alone in his house.

He had to feed himself, clean the house and find some way of laundering his clothes.

He was desperate for attention because there was no one there to listen to him and his imagined troubles, so he told our family and friends that it was my entire fault that he was so terribly upset.

Because he is such a convincing liar, they believed him, and a few people wouldn't speak to me.

This meant that not only had he given me a lifetime of abuse and neglect—-always behind locked doors where there was never a witness, lived on my family's money and resources, (including not having a job for the best part of twenty years), he tried his level best to turn our family and friends against me by blaming me for his present misfortune—leaving me as isolated and vulnerable as he could.

Again, he had no thought or compassion for me or my feelings, which demonstrated that he only looked upon me as a meal ticket, and when that meal ticket was withdrawn, he didn't know where to turn for comfort.

He didn't have a washing machine and asked if I would do his washing until he got one fixed in. This was a small price to pay for having him living a couple of miles away, so I agreed, and did for almost a year.

My little house was heaven. There was no one to boss me around and try to make me do anything that I didn't want to do.

Luckily, I could always amuse myself, sewing, decorating, gardening, drawing, painting etc.

I valued my freedom very highly.

It was like a big, new, sweet toy that protected me, and I could come and go as I pleased without questions.

No 'mind games', just peace, restfulness, and being left to have my own thoughts rather than have them constantly invaded by his endless, inane chattering about how good he was at out—witting the world.

I eventually joined a singles group, Nexus, to make new friends that had never heard of him, and begin new and—hopefully—diverse interests.

This proved to be the case, and within a little while, one of the men, Lewis, proved to be a good gentle, fun-loving friend, and, although we had vastly differing backgrounds, we seemed to have the same outlook on life, and shared a slightly wicked sense of humour.

I was happier than I'd been for years and years, and felt as though a huge load had been lifted from my shoulders. I gradually acquired a circle of friends that didn't know my previous life, so I was rid of the reminders when I was with them.

Lewis and I went out together a few times and began to get to know each other.

For me, being with him was like coming across a calm, tranquil, peaceful lake, after being in turmoil and lost in a wild, scary, dangerous forest.

He was a highly intelligent, self-employed, university educated scientist, a man that enjoyed freedom and independence, and showed me that I could enjoy those qualities too.

He introduced me to lots of exciting things that were new to my hitherto, sheltered world.

Morris dancing, singing clubs, bird watching and archaeology amongst others, and whatever happens in the future, I shall always be grateful to him for helping me out of my cage!

My ex-husband got wind of this, and because he was still trying his best to jealously keep tabs on me, he also joined Nexus!

As soon as I made this discovery, I gave the details to Head Office, and, after they had checked my story with the police, they banned him from the organisation.

An action for which I am deeply grateful!

Thank you, Nexus

This didn't stop him from challenging me about my new man friend one day when he came to pick up his washing.

We had been divorced for well over a year and a half, but the thought of me being friendly with another man still incensed him.

He began to question me about our relationship, and I could see that whatever my answers were, his mind was already made up, because he, as usual, didn't listen to me, and his premeditated actions were speedily forming in his head.

He flew into an instant, volatile, bad-temper tantrum, shook me violently by my shoulders, and hit my head with his hands, one after another, twice with each hand, very hard, knocking my head from side to side and sending my glasses flying across the room.

I screamed at him, ran into the hall, managed to grab the bag with his washing in, and open my front door. I then threw it as hard and far as I could outside onto the front lawn, held the door open, and shouted at him to get out and leave me alone.

This he did, and by the time he'd picked his laundry up off the grass, he'd realised just what he'd done, became frightened that he'd burnt his boats regarding being friends with me ever again, and started to say how sorry he was, and that it would never happen again.

This he did, but he said it to himself, because I slammed the door as soon as he went through it.

I could still hear him however, and remained as still and quiet as I could until he pulled his car out of my drive.

I was just glad to still be alive, but distraught, devastated, feeling very vulnerable and alone

He drove off, leaving me hurt, crying, trembling and unsure what to do next.

As much as the physical damage he had caused me, he had damaged my very own privacy in my own home which I'd never had whilst I was married.

Violated my basics rights, once again…

I was very shocked and knew that I daren't risk him coming into my house and beating me again.

I had to have some sort of protection, and because I had always kept quiet about his bad temper, abuse and anti-social behaviour, there was no one I could turn to.

It's difficult to tell friends and family the truth, when you've been forced to be quiet about it for years...they just don't believe it.

So, I had no alternative but to ring Braintree Police for advice, something that I should have done years and years ago.

They were extremely understanding, helpful and listened to me carefully, gave me lots of assistance by letting me know that they were firmly on my side.

He had left a message on my answering machine, saying how sorry he was and would never do it again.

Thus, for the first time ever, he gave me evidence for the police.

They also said that he had overstepped the mark by miles on this incident alone and that I could prosecute him immediately. I declined to do this, because I didn't want my daughters to have their father dragged through the courts, but the knowledge that I finally had professional help, was so welcome, supportive and comforting.

This gave me the confidence to ban my ex-husband from ever coming to my house again.

At last, the police do take domestic violence seriously.

He still hasn't bought a washing machine, but now relies on our youngest daughter to do it for him, even though his woman friend of the moment has a laundry in the family and he helps her with it!

But he always has to have that degree of control over somebody...

Will I ever be free from him?

Do It and Be Damned!

After the divorce, I really thought that my life had settled down. But this proved to be wrong for I had reckoned without my stalker and potential killer!

I had my own fully-paid for little house and car, modest savings and an enjoyable part-time job in the art department of Hannays' in Braintree, the town where I live. The two-family owned shops, one sells craft, art, needlework and gifts, the other is a book shop, has been well-established for fifty years. A very traditional concern, not a bar code in sight, with an Olde Worlde atmosphere, and a strong, old fashioned emphasis on help, reliability, supply and civility that has served the town well for all the time it's been there.

The policy works wonderfully and is much tried and trusted.

Customers come to us from miles around in the knowledge that Hannays' is reliable, consistent and will do their best to oblige happily and willingly.

With the result that we are always, consistently on the go.

The girls are good to work for and with, all helpful, and, as it's a very busy shop everybody has to pull their weight. This encourages us to think alike regarding the business, and each other. An excellent bonding situation and quite unique in these days of fast service, faceless and soulless establishments.

So it is easy and pleasurable to be there, if only on a regular part-time basis.

Apart from the times that my stalker comes in!

He knows full well that I won't argue with him in front of the staff and customers there, so he can enjoy the false effect of friendship from me.

But trust, support and loyalty underpin all our relationships, and those qualities have hardly ever been mutually present between us.

Sometimes, he walks around the town until he finds where I've parked my car...

He texts, rings and tries all ways to contact me, saying that he can't live alone and will do anything to have me back.

He is my ex-husband who can't let go and is still haunting me.

I'm going to have to really give him the heave-ho to rid myself of him.

There's a saying in Yorkshire that goes, "You can't shake shit off a blanket!"

I am that blanket, quite determined not to be covered in his excrement for all my life and will have to risk taking strong, drastic action in a last-ditch effort to be finally free...

This is why I have had to write some hitherto dark, secret events down, to let the story be known, and to show everyone why I can no longer tolerate, shield or protect him.

It's as though I've been a psychiatric nurse for the best part of forty years, which has taught me so much about human behaviour.

I had to watch his face and body language at all times, to anticipate his mood and reaction to situations in order to diffuse them before conflict arose. More often than not, he was automatically acting, because it's a natural way of life for him, therefore, the words that he spoke did not reflect his underlying motive.

So as to avoid having an argument, in which he could immediately turn violent, I learned to read the signs and act accordingly—either to smooth his easily ruffled feathers or remove the obstacle that he couldn't immediately deal with—whether real or in his imagination.

So it was a huge, learning, curving and climbing process for me, which I'd like to share...

But I know now that the patient has grown far too dangerous for me to deal with by myself, and that he has no hope of recovery.

He can't change his nature, any more that he can change the natural colour and shape of his body, hair or eyes.

He knows when he does wrong, but gets a kind of sick pleasure from accomplishing control, even though he recognises that other people don't behave this way, and that he doesn't conform with the great majority of us.

Yet another contributing factor that I firmly believe, is that because he received so much rejection from his mother, he thrives on it, as a childhood characteristic that is necessary in his life. So rejection to him is just a welcome normality, from which he gains satisfaction, a strange stability and without it, he feels deprived.

I now also firmly believe that he is waiting to be hit very hard, or locked in a dark pantry as his mother had done. Thus, in some sick way that is beyond my comprehension, he would relive a childhood scene with his mother that gives him the undivided attention that he craves.

This is why he feels a compulsion to repeatedly keep pushing and crossing that thin red line, that we all know divides right from wrong.

Also, the character is formed by the genes, totally inborn and couldn't possibly be changed permanently, although he has become exceedingly adept at copying other people and acting or mimicking decent behaviour for short periods.

Just long enough to lie his way through the day with smiling, joking charm and utter conviction into, or out of, any situation.

He can't sustain good behaviour for long however, without reverting to his norm, with which he feels comfortable and most happy.

But it's exceedingly upsetting and difficult for decent people to understand, as this involves his many, varied high and low mood swings, which are not easy to follow unless you've lived with them for years.

Most alien, disturbing, strange and puzzling for the vast majority of the population.

I can no longer handle him by myself.

I've grown accustomed to freedom, and I like it.

He's not going to get out of my life voluntarily, because he can't stand his own company for long, and has to have someone to bear the brunt of his way of life.

We all have to face our own demons sooner or later, and he'll have to find someone that will help to shoulder his intense insecurities and attempt to untangle his dramatic persona, or at least try to understand it...

So, through no fault of my own, after a lifetime of stressful struggling, I'm going to have to make a big effort to be free, for the sake of my health and safety.

Then, I'll have to face the consequences.

But I know I'll have to do it—and be damned...

To the silken ties that bind us,
To the tasks that fate assigns us,
To the path that lies behind us,
To each cause, that needs assistance,
To the future in the distance.
(Unknown author)

This is a copy of the final letter that I sent to him, almost five years after I divorced him for domestic violence.

He was still trying to keep tabs on me, by phoning, emailing, texting and refusing to take 'No!' for an answer.

Do You Believe Me Now?
I have told you for years that I couldn't bear to live with you, under any circumstances, but you never listened.

You are arrogant enough to believe that I still can't live without you—you are wrong.

Apart from my childhood, I have never been happier since I divorced you for a miserable lifetime of your venomous ways, masochistic secrets and domestic violence.

I value my newfound freedom extremely highly.

I have told you to 'Leave me alone!' in as many ways and as many times, as I could. Me swearing at you only seems to give you amusement. You don't pay attention or even listen to what I say at all.

Me telling you that the mere thought of you makes my flesh creep and the sight of you makes my stomach turn over, only makes you say that those feelings will soon pass, and you will continue to 'keep in touch' with me. This is called stalking by anyone else in the real world.

I can no longer bear the thought of being old, ill and frail, and having my last view of this world being you advancing towards me with a pillow, to 'put me out of my misery', in the same way as you instructed me to suffocate my father.

I would be very foolish to allow that to happen, in the light of all the dangerous threats, caustic cruelty and violence that you have shown to me.

I made it possible for you to 'retire' in luxury for the best part of twenty years, living in very comfortable and well-appointed houses, having a brand-new car every two years, excellent holidays and in return, you made me fight to defend myself, and be on my guard at all times.

I'd also like to gently remind you that when we met, you hadn't a clue about luxury living or even decent living, and everything you have now, came from my family and me.

It's payback time now, time to get out of my life, stop pestering, stalking and hounding me...!

This is your opportunity to move away, where they won't know about you, unless they read my book or know me personally, because I shall make your hateful violence, selfish ways and uncontrollable temper known to all as a warning.

I have to be free from you, and this is the only way I can do it, because you won't release me.

Terrorists can't be allowed to win.

Constance

And Finally

I have had to write my memories in this book because I suffered in silence and played the role of passive housewife for years, even shielding my daughters from the truth, now the story needs to be told, so that they at least, know the facts.

Society finds it difficult to see femininity as anything but submissive and passive at present.

Time will alter that, as independent, intelligent girls begin to push and break through the glass ceilings, but where these hidden pockets of control are allowed to continue in secret, it will take longer to change.

I would like this book to be a road to independence for all those girls, boys, women and men out there, who are being subjugated.

I know it's still happening because I've mentioned writing this book to a few people, and I've been surprised at the amount of response it's received.

Readers have confided their family secrets and problems to me, which they are doing their best to resolve, and/or tolerate.

It happens in all walks of life; rich or poor doesn't seem to make any difference, because it's the power of control that these freaks of nature feed voraciously on.

My friends were all surprised, some even horrified, when I got divorced.

They didn't know how tense, intimidating and antagonistic the situation had developed behind locked doors, where no one could see.

Psychopaths can be extremely charming, most engaging and very entertaining when out and about amongst 'normal' people.

The life and soul of a party.

But, when closeted, given the correct situation in the safety and privacy of their own home, they can be inflexibly belligerent and demanding, with an inability and unwillingness to tolerate minor frustrations.

No one takes bullying seriously.

That's a bully's attitude—they know that it's reliably true—so they intensify the abuse, and, when bullying goes unchecked, it increases because it's just a game to the aggressor.

More often than not, the victim is blamed…because that's easier than having to battle on behalf of someone, when, on the surface, and without any evidence, everything seems perfectly normal…but lack of evidence is no proof that it doesn't exist…

Bullies have to be named and shamed, to put a stop to their extremely unpleasant aggression, which, if not attacked with a powerful determination to conquer with absolute conviction, only grows stronger.

So this book is to tell the truth that has been denied to me for so long, and to help my family and friends understand my situation.

It is to help and support anyone in this position, and prove to them that there is a way out, and for the sake of their safety and health, they must find it

If your friends and family don't believe what's happening, there's a lot of good, solid, professional assistance out there, in the form of peer groups, Women's Aid, Women's Refuge, Police authorities and Social Services, so never be afraid to use them.

That's why they are there.

They exist to help you.

They have been created to attempt to stamp out domestic violence.

But until you find the strength to overcome your fear, bang your drum incessantly as loudly as you can. and tell them, they won't know...

Only you can do it—and If I Can, believe me, You Can!

If I Can, You Can!

This is to prove that I have read the book that Constance, my ex-wife, has written, which has the title named above.

All the events in it are quite true, although I don't like admitting it, and I can see how much I planned to scare her repeatedly.

However, I am now a reformed character, and will do my best to make up for the secret horrors which my terrorising behaviour put her through

Roy N Redmayne

Psychopaths—psychology—psychologist

Born that way—don't experience the same emotions as us, something missing in brain, like colour blindness.

Dangerous, without conscience.

Deeply damaging at home, spousal assault, versatile, manipulative, disruptive at work— 'what's in it for me?' attitude.

Public enemy number one—shallow, charming, remorseless, easily bored, anti-social, plausible liars, earnest apologisers, grudging sense of work.

Want/ need to be on a pedestal, narcissistic in all areas of society.

Ruthless lack of concern for others, engaging, no compassion, good actors. No empathy.

Inborn—genes don't work together properly

Not deprivation, because third world children haven't anything and don't turn out to be psychopaths.

Can't change, incurable, callous, parasitic, beguiling, engaging.

Inability to tolerate minor frustrations.

Failure to learn from past experiences.